SIGHTLINE

STRATEGIC PLANS
THAT GATHER MOMENTUM
NOT DUST

Rebecca Sutherns, PhD, CPF

Illustrations by Rosanna von Sacken, M.Sc., CPF

Illustrations by Rosanna von Sacken
Cover Design by Oliver Sutherns
Author Photo by Hilary Gauld-Camilleri
Edited by Mish Phillips and Stephanie Ayres

First published 2020 by Rebecca Sutherns and Hambone Publishing
www.hambonepublishing.com.au

For information, contact:
Rebecca Sutherns
rebecca@rebeccasutherns.com
www.rebeccasutherns.com

ISBN 978-1-9995761-3-4 (paperback)
ISBN 978-1-9995761-4-1 (ebook)

ENDORSEMENTS

"If you are truly looking for a new way to gain engagement and execution of your strategic plan, then *Sightline* is your nirvana. This is an experience-based collaborative approach to strategic planning that delivers results!"

— *Bruce Magee*, GBB Innovation

"Whether you are brand new to strategic planning, or battle-scarred after decades of scribbling on coloured sticky-notes, this book is for you. Rebecca Sutherns demystifies the planning process with welcome logic and practical rigour. If you are planning to plan then you owe it to the future of your organization to read *Sightline*."

— *Jonathan Bennett*, former CEO and Founder of Laridae

"*Sightline* captures the heart of a well thought out planning process. Rebecca Sutherns outlines the unspoken elements that gifted facilitators bring to the process. Her ability to articulate models in a clear manner will assist many organizations to develop a solid collaborative plan that doesn't just live on a 'shelf'."

— *Rachel Gooen*, Organizational Development Consultant, 5th House Consulting

"*Sightline* is a timely and relevant book, sure to become a must-read for leaders and board members in social profit organizations everywhere. Rebecca has generously shared her experiences, gained over years of facilitating strategic planning, leading organizations, community service, and success.

The reader is immediately drawn in by Rebecca's practical, unpretentious, and familiar writing style. We become part of her story as she talks about you, I and we, in a manner that inspires us to go further and deeper in creating new directions for our organization.

Especially creative are Rebecca's insights into exciting possibilities emanating from multi-agency planning. She challenges us to get with the program and move from seeing our individual organizations as unique. She clearly establishes future directions in recognizing opportunities for the reader to view causes from a systems level. Theories of Change are presently orphans in many social profits. Rebecca provides innovative ways in which to integrate the organization's Theory of Change into its strategic plan.

Sightline is easy-to-read, immensely practical, and, at the same time, futuristic. I highly recommend it to all levels of social profit leaders and board members."

— *Cathy Brothers*, CEO Capacity Canada

"Rebecca's book is a great mix of relevant theory, practical advice and action for building strategic plans that work. I particularly liked the inclusion of deliverables, decisions, key questions and steps outlining how to get there. A great tool kit for any organisation embarking on a strategic planning journey, whether it's the first time or a refresh of existing strategy."

— *Gary Austin*, Co-Founder & Facilitator, circleindigo

"Books on strategic planning often make a choice between providing a high-level justification of the need for a fulsome process or a practical guide to actually getting it done. In *Sightline*, Rebecca Sutherns effectively provides both in a single volume that is both thorough and useful. Consultants and facilitators will dig into the extensive theory behind the 6 A model, while those who are looking for direction on how to produce a real plan that is both well-conceived and flexible will be able to follow a path to exactly what they need."

– Chris Wignall, executive director of Catalyst Foundation and author of *The Reaction Dashboard*

"Ever read a great strategy business book but you needed to 'translate' it in your head for your clients? Finally, Rebecca Sutherns has written the strategic planning book for us. Wise questions will guide you to plan at the right scale. This is a practical, wise, jargon-free book, from an advisor who deeply understands this sector."

– Sam Bradd, author and facilitator, Drawing Change

GRATITUDE

I appreciate the many people who made this book possible and those who will make it worth having written by using it in their work. I am grateful to the clients who have entrusted me to join them on their strategy making journeys and who have referred me to others. Our shared learning made the creation of this resource possible. To the colleagues who read early drafts, improved later ones and made the finished product look beautiful, please accept my thanks. And to my sweet family who freed me up to write and pulled me away from it for dance parties at all the right moments, I am especially thankful.

Contents

WELCOME

Helping you decide if this book is for you

SIGHTLINE:

A visual axis,

a hypothetical line,

ideally unobstructed,

from someone's eyes to what is seen.

Welcome

Have you ever bought tickets to a concert or a sporting event that say "obstructed view"? Maybe that automatically rules them out for you. Or maybe the discounted price is worth it just to be there, even if you can't see very well. But you're always left with a twinge of regret, aren't you?

What about selecting a seat in the middle of the auditorium to enjoy your child's school concert, only to have a very tall parent sit directly in front of you? You spend the evening bobbing back and forth as that person moves their head, trying to maintain your view of your star of the show.

Or perhaps you've arrived at a lovely hotel room and peeled back the curtains, only to discover that your anticipated view of the water is mostly blocked by the high-rise next door.

We would all prefer an unobstructed view. Good visibility. A sightline.

Sightlines let us see the destination clearly. They show us what is possible.

But a view of the goal isn't enough, unless you simply plan to look at it. If your sightline is not toward a concert stage or a sunset, but rather involves a destination you wish to visit, you need a way to get there. Think of visiting a renowned coffee shop perched at the top of a mountain. You can see the place from ground level, but getting there looks intimidating. You need a pathway up that hill — ideally one that is well trodden. You might find that there is more than one way to get there; you'll appreciate having some clearly marked options along the way. And if you're lucky enough to encounter people who have successfully made the trek, are on their way back down, and are willing to share stories and a few tips, then your confidence will lift and your arrival will be virtually guaranteed. Inspiring sightlines can shift our belief in what is about to happen.

This is a book about strategic sightlines. It's about establishing a line of sight between where you are now and where your organization wants to be. And it's about mapping a route to get there with a group. It's a book about collaborative strategic planning. After all, strategy is perhaps the most important sightline of all, and it's only as strong as your ability to execute it. That never happens alone.

A strategic plan and the process of strategic planning are akin to having good visibility — a clear view of a worthy destination for your organization. Just as strategy is a sightline, so too is this book: it's a tool to help you clearly visualize where you want to go in terms of strategy making and helps you map out a way to get there. This book shows those who need and build strategic plans what is possible and proposes a series of steps to get there. It lays out not just *why* you should plan strategically, but *who* should do it, and *how*.

To me, solid strategic planning is not unlike vacation planning. You've chosen a destination you're excited about and travelling companions you enjoy; your GPS software is up to date; you know the stops you'd like to make along the way, and you're spending money you actually have. I love travel planning, but I have lots of friends who don't. Which still works out well — it just means I get to do it for them! Same thing here. This book will give you all the tools you need to do the planning yourself, but if it's just not your thing, you'll also find advice on asking for help from someone who is better placed to do it than you are. You can dive in to whatever depth suits you best.

A solid strategic plan articulates the impact you want to have in the world and aligns your activity with that intention. It also provides you with a rubric or filter that justifies saying no to numerous seemingly compelling opportunities so that you're free to say a strong yes to the few that *will* get you where you want to go within the timeframe you've laid out. It is about both change and continuity: it determines the desired direction, then stabilizes the organization to move toward it.[1] The problem is, most of the time we don't develop a shared strategic plan. We don't know what we're aiming for, our teams are aiming for different things, or equally frustrating, we know what we're aiming for, but we don't know how to get there.

There is more than one way to do strategic planning well. I am not dogmatic about following one particular model, but I do know that the design of the process generates a particular kind of plan, and that's why I think it is important to be intentional about that process. The process and the product are both important.

CONTEXT

I'm usually a big fan of starting with context. I could choose to begin this book with a description of all the big trends: what's going on with technology, the climate emergency, the economy, or any number of other elements of the zeitgeist that characterizes our world right now.

And yet.

I wrote this portion of the first draft of this manuscript on day 42 of staying at home during the COVID-19 global pandemic. It makes writing about strategic planning seem like a bit of an oxymoron when everything about our context has changed.

The irony is not lost on me that anything I might say about context could well be different by the time you read this book. Context does matter, but I'm not sure that the context of today matters very much for the context of tomorrow, at least not in terms of my describing a snapshot of that context to you here. It's stuff you probably already know, it will all be different very soon, and in any case you can get a more thorough treatment of it elsewhere.

So rather than beginning with a description of our collective context, I'm going to suggest that you pay close attention to *your* context and adapt what you read here to that context on an ongoing basis. This is your first step toward strengthening your strategic planning muscles.

While a global treatment of context may not be very helpful, what I can do is to say a few things about the context of strategic planning and facilitation that will situate and frame what comes next.

Strategic planning is commonly practiced, occasionally documented, but rarely researched. The recent academic literature on it is scant, though you can find mention of it in various adjacent fields. I will, of course, draw on some of it here where relevant. Books on the subject are primarily either MBA textbooks or of the kind commonly found on the business shelf at airport bookstores. The latter tend to be case studies or compilations thereof, or uninspiring variations on *Strategic Planning For Dummies*[2], often coming out of private sector experience. But for all their shortcomings these books are not without value, and I will look to them as well. While this book might be considered to fall into this same category, there is a critical difference, and that is in its practical application. This book won't just make the case for strategic planning in uncertain times, it will give you the tools to get it done in a way that perfectly suits your situation.

To this end, I am writing this book with all sectors in mind. Strategic planning in the private sector, the public sector, and the non-profit sector has key differences, but I'm writing from the perspective that the similarities are stronger than those differences. Unlike private organizations, public and non-profit organizations are relatively new to rigorous strategic planning. Strategic planning is also a bit more dynamic and challenging in the public and non-profit sectors, because the metrics of success are fuzzier. It's messier, but no less important. I have been involved in strategic planning exercises within and across each of these sectors, and I will draw on that experience in the examples provided throughout.

This book also sits inside a body of work on facilitation, as that is where my main expertise lies, based on more than two decades of providing facilitation service to clients. "Facilitation" is a term used in various ways across numerous settings. Here, I use it to mean a set of skills by which structured group conversations happen, usually leading to increased engagement and/or clearer decision-making. Not unlike strategic planning, facilitation happens in practice more than it is documented, and far more than it is rigorously researched. This book does draw on the wisdom of those who've come before me in the facilitation field — most often shared both in writing and in practice through the International Association of Facilitators[3], of which I have recently become the Regional Director for Canada.

Collaboration

My preference is for planning to be *collaborative*. As Lafley and Martin write in *Playing to Win,* "Any new strategy is created in a social context...strategy requires a diverse team with the various members bringing their distinct perspectives to bear on the problem. A process for working collaboratively on strategy is essential because all companies are social entities...people need to think, communicate, decide, and take action together, in order to accomplish anything meaningful."[4] According to Wolf and Floyd, "The achievement of strategic adaptation appears to depend on which actors are involved in strategic planning and how such participation is implemented."[5] In their review of public sector strategic planning, John Bryson and Lauren Hamilton Edwards note, there do not seem to be any strategic planning studies indicating when it might be advisable *not* to include stakeholders in... strategic planning.[6] Or more to the point, "there are very few — if any — public problems that can be solved without such collaboration."[7] Bill Staples makes this point even more fundamentally in *Transformational Strategy:* " The respect for the basic dignity of all human beings is a compelling reason for participatory approaches to decision making."[8]

It only takes a quick scan of the (fairly scant!) literature on collaboration to see that it's written from a variety of starting points. Some authors make the case for collaboration, while others take collaboration as their default setting. Dig a little deeper and you'll discover that even the word collaboration is open to interpretation: some authors define collaboration as participation inside an organization, while others use it to refer to joint participation across organizations or even sectors. In this book, I'm not going to be too specific about how we define collaboration. But I will say from the outset that I consider internal participation to be the low bar, the 'baseline' of collaboration.

You'll also see some limited literature quoted here on "collaborative strategic planning," where the meaning is across agencies — usually amongst branches within the public sector. I think multi-agency planning is at the leading edge of this field, and I look forward to watching it unfold. When this kind of collaborative planning happens, it often tends to be guided more by general principles than by specific goals and plans, mostly because the locus of control of the collaborative as a whole is limited by the fact that individuals have little influence over how a plan gets executed inside organizations for which they do not directly work. Collective impact case studies might offer the best insight into how more concrete, specific planning can happen across agencies.[9] Given this variation in collaborative scope, let's agree for now that collaborative strategy development, at a minimum, involves engagement internally. And if you're able to take it beyond that, perhaps initially to your immediate stakeholders, then to other agencies — and not just in shaping your own plan but also in developing joint, system-level plans — you are leading the way to a new frontier of community planning. I can only encourage you to document what you're learning so that the rest of us can benefit too.

Done well, collaborative strategic planning reduces blind spots and builds buy-in. As Jordan Tama found in his review of collaborative planning initiatives in the US public sector, "strategic planning and management processes are more effective when external stakeholders are more involved in them, and ... stakeholders are more likely to support such processes if they have a voice in them."[10] But collaboration is not always better. It is certainly not an end in itself. And it can sometimes make us less brave. We're inclined to listen to the most common perspectives rather than the most edgy or insightful ones, which can lead us to adopt "vanilla" strategies that look remarkably similar to what we have done before. My interest here is in mapping out a process that allows you to be better informed and more enthusiastic about your path forward, but also perhaps to be more courageous in the path you choose.

Collaborative decision making

Too often instructions about collaborative processes just assume that groups of people know how to make decisions together. I've said that strategy is about making choices, and it is. I've also said that I believe strategy should be done collaboratively, and I do. But the practice of making decisions in a group is rarely explicitly taught.

According to research quoted by Chip and Dan Heath in Decisive,[11] the process side of decision-making is six times more important than the analytical side. Good process leads to better analysis, but the reverse is not always true. I want to offer some guidance about how collaborative decision making itself can happen in a group, because without clarity around the process of collaborative decision making, groups can have an idea of what they're trying to do, but no clear idea of how to get there.

The first step is to be very clear about the decision you're trying to make or the dilemma you're trying to resolve. Everyone in the room needs to agree on what the problem actually is. Albert Einstein was onto something when he said, "If I had only one hour to save the world, I would spend fifty-five minutes defining the problem, and only five minutes finding the solution."

Second, is it obvious to everyone in the room why that problem is worthy of being solved? How will fixing it make a difference? In the context of this book, each step is in fact a collaborative decision to be made, all leading toward a fulsome and useful strategic plan. The benefits of having a strategy justify the effort. Dr. Max Mckeown warns that groups of people tend toward making easy decisions, even when those decisions don't solve valuable problems.[12]

Once you have a clear understanding of the decision to be made and why it's important, *the third step is to clarify decision rights.* Whose decision is this to make? Too often, people confuse being asked to participate in the decision-making conversation as being offered the right to make that decision. In the context of strategic planning, the people giving input may be different from the Steering Committee members, who are different again from the Board of Directors. Be clear where decision rights lie for which parts of the process.

The fourth step is to identify what inputs will inform the decision. If you are conducting an interview, that conversation might be one of many sources of information within a broader process that could also include, for example, comparative research, talking to people you trust, gauging public opinion, or hosting other, similar workshops. It helps the group to understand what else will be taken into consideration beyond the conversations in which they are participating.

Next, identify the options under consideration and what factors or assumptions would need to be true in order for each option to be successful. You don't want to jump too soon to defending a solution or fixing a problem without first being clear what the various possibilities under consideration are.

The sixth step involves setting criteria for making the decision. At this stage I often have the group "decide how to decide before deciding" by identifying "what would make a good decision good?" Too often groups want to jump to the decision at this stage, especially when a variety of options have been presented. People find themselves quickly becoming fans of one option over another. This is where skilled facilitation becomes important, as the facilitator can set a slower pace and make decision-making criteria explicit.

The final step is to decide on the process by which the criteria will be applied to the options. Will all criteria be weighted equally? Will the decision be made with the help of an external facilitator? Will all the input be made public and transparent, or will only the final conclusion be communicated? *The complexity of the decision-making process should be proportional to the decision being made.* For an inconsequential decision, you don't need to be systematic and thorough with each of these steps. But for a large, high-stakes decision, being systematic about the steps you follow will lead to a decision-making process that is robust, defensible, transparent, and memorable. Later, when people wonder how or why a decision was made, you will be able to describe the process, thereby increasing their confidence in the legitimacy of the decision.

This process design can be what I call "accordioned" — shrunken or extended to fit the scale of the decision being made.

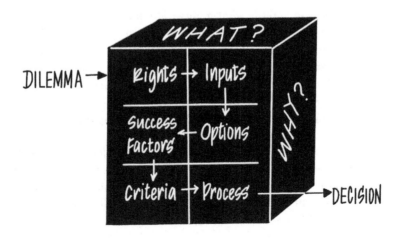

I am reminded of a tale told by my colleague Peter Cook[13] about his father, who said that if a team of smart, committed people couldn't reach a consensus within ten minutes, there were probably good arguments on both sides and you may as well toss a coin. Making no decision is worse than making a wrong one, and when there are strong arguments on both sides, there is no "wrong" one. Make it and move on.

Further planning principles

Before we move on, let me share a few additional principles about how strategic plans should be built.

First, your strategic plan should be *proportional* to the organization you're running. An unfortunate truth that I'm learning about strategic planning is that it takes almost the same amount of work for a small organization to build a plan as it does for a large organization, despite the smaller one having fewer resources at its disposal. So part of the challenge is working out how to keep your planning resources proportional to your overall budget, recognizing that there's a bunch of work to be done no matter how big or small you are. This book came out of that realization, after I received numerous requests for support from organizations that needed to do this work and weren't sure how, but could not afford an ongoing, long-term engagement with a strategic planning coach or consultant. It is my hope that this book will help you get your strategy done, within whatever resource constraints you're facing.

You will also notice that my approach to strategy development is *pragmatic*. There's no need to spend months doing something that should take weeks or days. I don't want you to get mired in unhelpful terminology. Visionary conversations are required and useful, but you also need to maintain momentum and get this thing done. There are lots of ways to do that well.

I believe that strategic planning should be *driven by decisions,* not just descriptions of how things are. Planning is ultimately about making choices, and this book will walk you through the series of choices you will need to make. Beyond that, it will coach you on how to lead a group through this decision-making process.

I also want to encourage you to develop a plan that is *flexible* over time. You do not have to be clairvoyant to develop strategy. Planning is not about being able to look into the future with certainty or predict it with accuracy. Nor does it rely on simple problems and a perfectly stable context in order to be successful. As Bryson et al. have noted, strategies are "both deliberately set in advance and emergent in practice."[14] Or, as Dr. Jason Fox asserts, strategic planning is about aligning your business model and business decisions with your context over time.[15] Hiroyuki Itami called this the "dynamic strategic fit" between external and internal factors and the content of your strategy.[16] Dr. Max Mckeown suggests that the "ultimate test of strategy is how successfully you are able to adapt yourself to circumstances and your circumstances to your desires."[17]

Perhaps most importantly, I think strategic planning should be *useful* and *yours*. Dr. Max Mckeown underscores the benefit of developing an organization that is hungry for change. Strategic planning is something you do, not because it's required or expected, but because you need it. The strategic planning police are not going to show up at your door asking to see your papers. This is *yours*. It should help *you*. There is no one right way to do it and no one correct outcome. It should reflect your unique organizational personality, in both its process and its outcome.

This book starts by making the case for why you need a strategy. Once you're there, it will help you actually get it done. And once it's done, it should sound and look just like you. Not only that, but it should clear the path toward successful implementation in real life.

IS THIS BOOK FOR YOU?

You are convinced you need a plan. You might even have some capacity to develop one. But maybe you want an understanding of what the scope of that assignment might be, or a roadmap and some company along the way. Or perhaps you've already engaged someone to accompany your organization on your planning journey, but you'd like an extra voice to triangulate their advice or provide a different route to get to the same goal. If any of this is ringing true, this book is for you, too. It sketches out multiple ways to get a plan done, helping you determine the particular blend of internal and external resources that's most appropriate for you.

Or maybe you're someone who says, "I know planning is part of my role, but I have no idea how to do it. I'm more of a 'fly by the seat of my pants' kind of leader. But that's not going over well with my board! I thought strategy was *their* job… yet they don't seem engaged enough to know that, let alone do anything about it. And have you seen the sorry state of my budget?" There are all kinds of reasons and excuses that might get in the way of actually building the kind of strategy you want. This book will show you how to push past them. In his book *Quick and Nimble*, Adam Bryant cites a study from Google which asserts that effective strategy setting for a team is a key behavior of an effective manager.[18] Whether you're a manager strategizing, whether you're strategizing for your whole organization or for your department or team, I hope that you'll find this book a helpful resource. It's a practical guide to building strategy that will help you make and stick to decisions.

Perhaps you lead a small organization that does not have the resources to hire an external consultant to support your strategy development process. This book is perfect for you, as its tips, tools, and activities will guide you to pull together a "DIY strategy" that meets your needs.

This is also a book for facilitators who support organizations in their strategic journeys. I trust it will give you some practical tools for use "in the room" — activities and "mini-scripts" to describe succinctly what you do and why it's important.

Or perhaps you're an organizational leader who is not convinced that you need a strategic plan. You've done fine without one, or the ones you've had in the past have proven to be irrelevant. Or maybe you used to be a fan, but you're no longer sure that strategic planning makes any sense at all, with the world as unsettled and unpredictable as it has ever been. If so, this book is for you, as it maps out a case for the value of strategic planning in today's uncertain context and lets you decide for yourself whether you're convinced enough to proceed.

This book comes out of my experience working with hundreds of organizations on their strategic planning processes over the past 25 years as a facilitator and trusted advisor. My experience is deepest in the community benefit sector, supporting medium to large non-profits, health organizations, post-secondary institutions and local governments, so you'll find that the examples in this book come largely out of those spaces. I also work with private sector firms that are seeking to build their communities.

If you're in a for-profit business that's looking at a triple or quadruple bottom line, the conversations in this book will resonate as you wrestle with how to describe and measure the social, environmental, workplace, and financial benefits of your work. And even if you aren't, you will find the encouragement here to be strategic, focused, and highly relevant to your context. Financial metrics of success such as revenue, profitability, and productivity might be more clearly defined in a for-profit setting than in a non-profit one. Non-profit planning requires different conversations to figure out what vocabulary to use and define metrics of success. Planning exercises in non-profits usually involve a volunteer board (loosely accountable to members), which introduces a different dynamic than in the private sector, where a board is usually paid or non-existent, or the public sector, where staff answer to council, voters, and residents. Public sector accountabilities have been described as "often diffuse and conflicting."[19] My intention here is to speak to the planning challenges in each of those settings.

You can read this book in multiple ways. It's accessible in bite-size chunks, so that you can refer to sections as you need them. Think of it as a coaching guide to reassure you or help you navigate along the way. You can check in at the stage most relevant to you. If you need to sell the why of a plan, perhaps to your board or even to yourself, turn to the section in which I outline the benefits of planning. If you are curious whose job it is to lead strategy development or who should be tasked with getting it done, there's a section for that, too. Perhaps you're curious about the outputs or deliverables you'll end up with, and who the audiences could be for those, and yes, you guessed it, there's a section for that as well. If you need a roadmap of how to create a strategic plan, you can turn to that section, remembering that there is always more than one way to get it done. Often when you see one way, it helps you devise your own customized path. If you need a granular description of how to run planning meetings — specific questions to ask at different stages and even mini-scripts to help clarify your wording — you can turn to that section. If you've already decided to hire an outside facilitator, you might choose to jump away from those how-to facilitation segments and toward the sections on how to develop your metrics of success, or how to communicate or implement the plan. Perhaps you need clarity about the quality checks that can be inserted along the way and at the end to confirm that you've implemented your plan effectively. For that, turn to the **Assess** section.

When we take what's in our heads and make it visible, we realize there's a lot there! What a great lesson for all of us in the way we approach meetings and working with our teams. The risk, of course, is that the process I'm describing can grow to be unwieldy (both in a book and in real life!). It can become way too complex, out of proportion to the importance of the task or the resources available to complete it. So, as we go along, I want to find ways to accommodate every kind of reader: those of you who want extensive detail, and those of you who just want the overview, the quick basics. Mastery is not always about understanding every last aspect of a process. Sometimes it's about making decisions for your own context, skill level, and interest level; about knowing how to prune and pare down information for use in your own setting.

A couple of years ago one of my strategic planning clients decided to take my two-day facilitation skills course. Not only that, she invited her entire team to participate. I thought to myself, "Well, I'm glad they all signed up, because that will be the last time they hire me to do any facilitation for them. Now they will all be trained to do it as well as I can." In fact, the opposite happened. Since realizing all of the thinking and skills that go into facilitation, they have in fact called me more often, because now they appreciate the nuances of this craft even more. I wonder if this book will actually do the same thing. Some of you will riffle through it and say, "Wow, that's too much. I don't want to become an expert at this. I'm going to hire an expert instead." Others will delight in the level of detail, and incorporate many of my tips into your own practice. My point is neither to work myself out of a job nor into more jobs. It's to provide a useful resource to allow every reader to decide for themselves how best to create and implement a strategic plan.

WHAT

Establishing a clear and shared understanding of what strategic planning is and what you'll hold in your hand and your head when you're done

What

Have you ever played on a team that used its own special terms to communicate quickly with one another? Or does your family have certain words that are unique to you? My kids can each recount stories of times they used "inside words" outside of our home, only to find out that the term was not understood beyond the bounds of our dinner table! Similarly, one of the things I find most useful when I work with groups is to establish common vocabulary. It becomes a kind of shorthand that accelerates our work together. Whether that language carries on outside of our session or not, at the very least it becomes temporarily useful in getting things done. It also creates a bond, a sense of togetherness, from having this unique shared vocabulary.

This section serves that purpose. It gives us a set of shared terms to build understanding and speed up our work. I'll address what strategic planning is and what to keep in mind as you embark on your planning journey in order to do it well. Here and throughout the book, you may find that others use different terms for similar things. More power to them! My goal is simply to frame how terms will be used in the context of our time together here, not so much to "get it right" but rather to "get it done."

STRATEGIC PLANNING 101

My starting point for this book is the premise that doing things out loud and on purpose is a good idea, and that strategic planning is a prime occasion for doing so. Teamwork is both helped and helpful when we make things explicit and deliberate.

Consider the matrix below. When we function at the low end of the "on purpose" scale, we are on autopilot, living according to our default settings. Life feels inconvenient and riddled with interruptions because we are always on the back foot, in reactive mode. Often, we feel as if life "happens" to us, as if we have no control over where life "takes us". When we live low on our out loud scale, we tend to hide things, even from ourselves. We forget that what seems obvious to us may not be obvious to others. When we are low on both intentionality and explicitness, we can feel unseen or even victimized. On the other end of the spectrum, the candor and intention that come from dialing up our behavior on both scales allow us to move into the "impressive" territory of being explicitly deliberate.

OUT LOUD & ON PURPOSE

INTENTIONAL

Insidious   Impressive

——————————————————→ EXPLICIT

Invisible   Inconvenient

- When we're neither intentional nor explicit, we're hiding even from ourselves.
- When we're intentional but not explicit, we can come across as insidious.
- When we're explicit but not intentional, we feel like life is happening to us.
- When we are both intentional and explicit, we are impressive and well respected.

DEFINITIONS

Simply put, strategic planning is the process by which your organization decides where it's going and how best to get there, over a certain period of time. Let's look briefly at other ways to describe it so we can pull out some common elements:

Henry Mintzberg, a prolific writer in the field of strategy making, refers to strategy as being about the interrelationships between decisions.[20] Dr. Max Mckeown, author of *The Strategy Book*, describes it as "connected, cumulative tasks that are worth more than the sum of their parts."[21]

Other writers describe it this way:

"Strategy is an integrated set of choices that uniquely positions the firm in its industry so as to create sustainable advantage and superior value relative to the competition."[22]

"[Strategic planning is] a deliberative, disciplined effort to produce fundamental decisions and actions that shape and guide what an organization ... is, what it does, and why."[23]

"[Strategic planning is] a more or less formalized, periodic process that provides a structured approach to strategy formulation, implementation, and control. The purpose of strategic planning is to influence an organization's strategic direction for a given period and to coordinate and integrate deliberate as well as emerging strategic decisions."[24]

Common elements of these definitions will serve as helpful reminders as you get started on your strategic journey:

- Strategic planning is fundamentally about making decisions.
- Strategy underscores the "why" behind your organization's existence and its key choices.
- Strategy is about setting your destination, your route, and your pace.
- Strategic planning should be intentional and cyclical.
- The components of a strategic plan should work together.

Notice that these elements describe the why, what, and how of strategy making.

Strategic planning is about setting your DESTINATION, your ROUTE and your PACE.

THE FIVE A'S OF STRATEGIC QUALITY

I will outline a more detailed rubric for checking the quality of your strategy, but it's always useful to begin with the end in mind. So here are five principles, or quality checks, to keep in mind as you develop your plan. These "five A's" should be used to guide the early decisions you and your team need to make before the real planning can begin. They provide the initial scaffolding for ensuring your strategy is robust. Later, we'll explore our core model, which has six A's instead of five. If these first A's provide the scaffolding, the six A's model is the skyscraper we're going to build inside it.

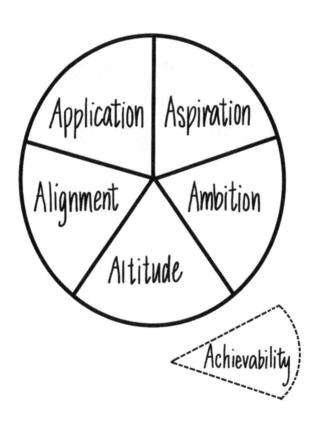

The first element is Aspiration. You need to be clear what a win looks like for your organization. What are you going after? This can be addressed in very broad terms — what is the change your organization is seeking to make in the world? Equally, it could be related specifically in terms of the deliverable(s) you want at the end of the strategic planning process. The former is often clearer in private sector firms (i.e. share value; profitability; market share) than in public or non-profit contexts, but in either case, clarity around definitions of success is critical. Think about it this way: when you are done with the planning process, what do you want to be holding in your hand? What do you want to have learned? What do you want to have experienced or felt?

The second A is Ambition. From the outset, you should be clear how ambitious your plan is seeking to be. In risk-averse cultures, such as most public sector agencies, radically ambitious strategic plans are rare. Bryson et al. describe public sector planning as "incremental-ism guided by an overall sense of direction." [25] Private sector and some non-profit organizations, on the other hand, are often more likely to live by the old adage, "no risk, no reward." Whatever your organization's attitude, it is critical to agree on the level of risk and ambition you intend to take on *before* you develop the details of your goals. Will this plan primarily describe where you are now, or where you want to be? Are you and your team looking for a radical revamp, or just a slight tweak of what you already do? Will the plan incorporate everything you do, or just the new, shiny stuff? Are you looking to set goals of the "moonshot" variety, or are you fine with a more modest action plan? These are all critical aspirational questions, and if you can ensure that your team members have answered them in similar ways before you begin developing your plan, the process and eventual outcomes are likely to be more satisfying.

The next component is Altitude. The level of detail should be con-sistent throughout your plan. You and your group may be tempted sometimes to fly at 40,000 feet and other times to dive right down to ground level. To mix my metaphors, many groups find themselves stuck in the weeds too much of the time, discussing specific tactics or projects or current annoyances, when they need to stay appropriately strategic. In some individual conversations, it's appropriate to alternate back and forth between high-level considerations and operational details, but at the end of the day, the finished strategic plan should be consistent in its altitude. That altitude should be fairly high — lower than your Mission and Vision and your Articles of Incorporation, but certainly higher than your annual plans, divisional responsibilities, or departmental project to-do lists.

The fourth check is Alignment. Your plan should eventually be aligned both vertically and horizontally. Vertical alignment means your measures of success link to your objectives, which link to your goals, which link to your mission (and back again!). Horizontal alignment means what's happening in one division or department is synergistically linked to what's going on in others, so that you can work together to achieve your organization-wide strategic intents. Strategic planning should not be done in functional silos, assuming that actions taken in one area of the organization will not affect another. Checking your vertical and horizontal alignment gives your plan integrity in both directions.

The final A is Application. My husband Tim is an engineer. He holds a Bachelor of Applied Science, where "Applied" suggests that it is practical and useful for solving real-life problems. The same should apply (no pun intended!) to your strategic plan. Successfully achieving it should actually matter! If you manage to do everything your plan says and only what your plan says, within the timeframe you've set, it should make a difference in the world. If the plan is not compelling, or if its impact is not meaningful, then it is not worth the time it will take to write it all down, let alone implement it. As Bryson et al. assert, "if commitment to a strategic plan is important, then strategic planning should be undertaken only when it can serve some useful purpose; otherwise, and unsurprisingly, any resulting strategic plan will likely have little impact."[26]

I could have added one more A to this model. When I ask groups to identify their number-one criterion for ensuring their emerging strategic plan is a good one, they inevitably suggest *Achievability*. While it's true that your plan ultimately needs to be implementable in real life, I trust you can see the critical interplay with application and ambition here. Your goals should be meaningful and inspiring. A plan you describe primarily as "achievable" may be entirely too modest. If it seems achievable already, is it really propelling you forward beyond your status quo? I would have loved to be at the table when the idea of 24-hour delivery by drone was first introduced at Amazon. I am quite sure there were some skeptics. Clearly achievability was not high on their list of strategic filters, thankfully. As Dr. Max Mckeown puts it, strategy can help you "use what is possible now to do things in the future that are impossible now."[27]

Making the case for collaborative strategy making in uncertain times and why it's worth the effort

Why

Strategic planning is often seen as a necessary evil — something you're *supposed* to do, rather like eating your leafy greens. It is seen as something you won't enjoy, and the results of which may or may not be worth the investment. I'm out to change your mind about that.

Ultimately, strategic planning should result in improved organizational performance. Unfortunately, there is no conclusive research demonstrating a direct relationship between planning and performance. Strategic planning does, however, contribute significantly to other mediating factors that help determine performance, such as organizational decision making, integration, and coordination.[28]

These mediating factors are critical. My experience working with hundreds of organizations over more than two decades has me convinced that collaborative strategic planning should be seen as an opportunity rather than an obligation. It is well worth the investment, as it strengthens the quality of your organization, your people, and your decisions.

REASONS

Here are 14 reasons why:

Your *organization* becomes:

1. Responsive
2. Credible
3. Accountable
4. Collaborative

Your *people* become:

5. Invested
6. Well-informed
7. United
8. Well-led

Your *decisions* become:

9. Relevant
10. Intentional
11. Explicit
12. Filtered
13. Defensible
14. Aligned

A collaboratively created strategy helps **your organization** to be:

1. Responsive

This may seem counterintuitive. Some people avoid developing a strategic plan because they don't want to be tied down by it. They fear being locked in. Yet the opposite is true. The best improvisers, in music or dance, are the ones with the most rigorously practiced technique. Not only does creativity thrive within constraints,[29] but it's only in knowing you are choosing to go off course that you can assess whether the deviation is wise or not. Having a strategy allows you to knowingly deviate from it. But you can't take a detour if you never set your path to begin with. If you've ever taken a road trip, you already know that deciding to take the scenic route is very different from losing your way.

2. Credible

The process of creating a new strategic plan gives you a reason to make contact with the people who care about your work, both internally and externally. If you've been looking for an excuse to get in front of your funders or investors, this is it. It reminds them you exist. It offers another touchpoint, thereby building your relationship with them. It gives you a reason for a high-quality conversation that is not about asking for money. At least, not directly. But people are far more willing to give money to organizations with vision. As Peter Senge said, "It's not what the vision is, it's what the vision does!"[30] It positions you as a partner that is taking the long view and working to stay relevant. It builds your brand.

For your staff, too, the planning process offers an opportunity for engagement across all levels and sites of the organization. It positions you as a leader who does not have all the answers, who is willing to accept feedback and share power — and that increases your currency with them. The co-creation process builds organizational goodwill across all of your stakeholders.

3. Accountable

When you develop a strategic plan, you commit to a set of performance metrics that are no longer only in your own head. By putting
those targets out into the world, you are inviting others to hold you
accountable to them. It ups your game. To return to the blind spot
metaphor we used earlier: Not only do we need to see who's driving in our blind spot, but having to do so makes us a better driver!
Here's the bonus: vulnerability is in fact proactive. By articulating
your targets, you actually become more likely to achieve them. Some
studies show that when we write a goal down, our chances of achieving it go up by 42%! Writing a goal down in detail and reading it
regularly encodes that content in our brain, helping us remember it
more thoroughly and for longer, and also leads us to think in more
detail about how to accomplish it.[31] Strategic planning provides a
structured framework for doing this.

4. Collaborative

Developing a plan collaboratively sets the kind of culture and builds
the kind of skills that are likely to benefit your organization in the
future. One client of mine in the health and social services sector
invested several months in developing an internal strategic plan. The
process, which involved many conversations, workshops, and rounds
of edits by various members of the board and staff team, created
remarkably strong buy-in to the plan. But it did much more than that.
It also cut their teeth on collaborative work, which allowed them
to see the possibilities afforded by working collectively across sites
not only inside their organization, but outside it, too.

This organization had always worked in partnership with other
organizations, but now they began to take bolder steps. They sought
funding to create a strategic plan across multiple agencies. Their
Board of Directors started talking to other boards, and began to see
their mission — to better the community — collectively, rather than
trying to protect their own turf. And these changes led to a variety
of other impacts. A funder noticed their collaborative effectiveness
and offered them a sizable unsolicited grant. They saw tangible service

improvements, including reduced wait times and easier system navigation for clients and patients. And ultimately, they gained access to more resources, which allowed them to hire more staff. You can never quite predict the ripple effects of a commitment to collaboration.

Your strategic planning process, which is likely to be primarily inward facing to begin with, gives you an opportunity to practice productive collaboration. Having experienced collaboration that works, you can then turn those skills outward and apply them across your sector or community to expand your impact even further. Doing so positions your organization as a community builder, which in turn attracts additional resources and multiplies your impact.

A collaboratively created strategy helps **your people** to be:

5. Invested

Former Governor General of Canada David Johnston recounts how revolutionary it was for Canadian commanders to give each soldier the battle plan at Vimy Ridge in 1917. He writes of the transformative power of listening and inclusion in building trust. He affirms the importance of "inviting people to dance, not just to the dance"[32] and attributes a great deal of his success in his role to having a strategic plan, developed through a participatory process that included his entire staff. He understood something that has since been empirically proven: people are more likely to get behind decisions they had a part in making. Strategic plans are basically a series of decisions, rolled out over time. Successful implementation of those plans is therefore far more likely to occur when the people expected to carry them out have had a part in shaping them from the outset. Neuropsychologists confirm that "individuals demonstrate better memory for material they've generated themselves than for material they've merely read."[33] In his book The Process Matters, Joel Brockner draws on various studies to confirm that employees demonstrate greater commitment to decisions made using fair and inclusive processes.[34] Similarly, Chip and Dan Heath suggest that although decision-making processes aren't glamorous, when they are trustworthy they offer a confidence and boldness that would not be available otherwise.[35]

6. Well-informed

The organizational learning that occurs during a collaborative planning process can be immense. The learning process is a significant mediator in strengthening the link between strategy and performance, as long as participants don't become overloaded.[36] Through this process they gain a greater appreciation of all aspects of the organization, becoming more aware of what their colleagues do. They clarify their own opinions and benefit from hearing others' perspectives. They better understand the trade-offs inherent in choices. Planning also builds skills in thinking strategically, particularly for people who are not usually required to do so. This is but a glimpse of why the planning process itself can be as beneficial as its outcomes. They also underscore the need to continually communicate both the contents of the plan and its rationale to new people joining the team, so that they too can develop a sense of ownership over its content.

7. United

Any shared experience, especially one that requires some struggle over a period of time to produce something useful, strengthens the bonds between participants. Can strategic planning be fun? I think it can be. (Or at least better than people expect!) It gives your staff an opportunity to work across departments in new ways. It provides a new, shared vocabulary that contributes to a sense of collective understanding. Also, choosing to co-create such a significant document with your people signals to them that you value their input. It contributes to a positive culture.

8. Well-led

Strategy provides clarity and propels action. It helps you move through paralysis and overload to a place of conviction. Likewise, your team can transition from powerlessness and feeling overwhelmed to performing with confidence. As Henry Mintzberg notes, "Visionaries cannot always be found ... then the organization in need of a new strategy may have no choice but to learn collectively."[37]

Where does your team sit on the clarity ladder? Have a look at the following image. Knowing where you're at is the first step to moving up the ladder.

THE CLARITY LADDER

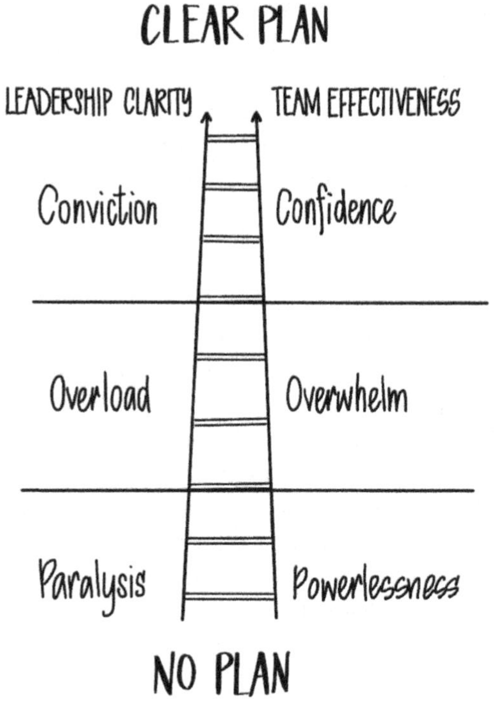

CLEAR PLAN

LEADERSHIP CLARITY   TEAM EFFECTIVENESS

Conviction   Confidence

Overload   Overwhelm

Paralysis   Powerlessness

NO PLAN

Finally, a collaboratively created strategy helps **your decisions** to be:

9. Relevant

One of the primary benefits of collaborative planning is that it reduces blind spots. When someone is driving in your blind spot, you need to change your speed or look from a different angle. The same is true in planning. No one person has all of the information or answers, particularly in today's context of increasing pace and complexity. As H. E. Luccock said, "No one can whistle a symphony."[38] A collaborative planning process gives you a structured opportunity to elicit the knowledge held by others and use it in service of your organization's success. We tend to think we are brighter, faster, stronger than we really are.[39] Yet blind spots are so named for a reason — no matter how clever we think ourselves to be, we can't see them! Multiple perspectives are protective against that kind of hubris. They keep your strategy well informed and relevant.

10. Intentional

By thoughtfully documenting your plans, you turn off organizational autopilot. You decide based on the best available information, instead of being carried along or repeating past patterns simply because "that's the way we've always done it." You act deliberately instead of by default. Making decisions based on our defaults, which are, by definition, "selected automatically unless a viable alternative is specified," results "in a reasonable, risk-averse strategy very similar to previous iterations."[40] When we act intentionally, we instead consider options and make reasoned choices. But we can only make conscious choices amongst those options of which we are aware. In *Living Forward,* Michael Hyatt refers to living intentionally as "putting the rudder back on a drifting boat."[41] Even if things don't end up as planned (and we know they won't!), you can address the unexpected from a position of agency and choice.

11. Explicit

There's a TED talk I've watched dozens of times. It's called *"Got a wicked problem? First, tell me how you make toast."*[42] I like it for a very particular reason: it demonstrates that even though we use similar words and even perhaps share some elements of experience, the images we hold in our heads of the same concept can vary — sometimes wildly. Even for something as mundane as making toast. (Watch the talk: when asked to draw toast, some people draw a toaster, some the jam, some a frying pan or a campfire or even wheat fields!) So it's worth checking in that we're actually picturing the same thing when we use the same words. Collaborative planning gives us a structured opportunity to do so. If we can't even agree on what making toast looks like, how likely are we to hold the same mental models for less concrete terms such as "mission," or "purpose," or "impact," or "priority?" It's through the planning process that we create space for dialogue, to help us compare out loud or visibly our images for the shared terms we use. Well-facilitated planning makes our thinking explicit, to one another and even to ourselves.

12. Filtered

Having a strategic plan allows you not only to articulate what you plan to do, but also to capture what you have ruled out. It gives you a tool for saying "no." And in this age of information overload and fake news, simply saying "no" with clarity and conviction can be powerfully liberating.

Strategy is a self-imposed set of limits. It shows you have done the difficult work of pruning. Greg McKeown refers to this task as an emotional rather than cognitive one.[43] Anyone who has moved house can relate to this. Packing takes longer than it should because there are choices to be made along the way about objects to which you have emotional ties. Once you've decided what to bring along, the packing process is far faster. Zig Ziglar wisely said, "The first step to getting what you want is having the courage to get rid of what you don't."[44] Similarly, David Maister argues, "Strategy is deciding whose business you are going to turn away."[45] Your plan is your editor. It provides a lens through which to evaluate opportunities and a rationale for turning most of them down. As Adam Richardson writes, "Beautiful, brutal clarity is your goal."[46] Once finished, your plan acts as the single decision that eliminates the need to make 1,000 other ones.[47] As Oliver Wendell Holmes Jr. said, "I would not give a fig for the simplicity this side of complexity, but I would give my life for the simplicity on the other side of complexity."[48]

13. Defensible

Your plan gives you a ready-made rationale for your decisions, a consistent script by which to justify your choices. A robust plan can be very helpful in quieting the voice of indecision or minimizing the impact of unwanted disruptions because it reminds you not only of what was decided, but why. Your strategy acts just like the mini-scripts used by salespeople to help close a deal. Mini-scripts capture patterns to help the speaker handle frequent scenarios without thinking. So too, your strategy speeds things up because not only do you not have to rethink the choice each time, you don't have to consider how best to explain it either. And even if you're not in a situation of having to justify your rationale to others, you may well need it for yourself every once in a while!

14. Aligned

Having a clear plan makes it more likely that your behaviors will be aligned with your intentions. And isn't that the very definition of integrity? When our mission cascades into goals that are in turn associated with actions and metrics, we are better equipped to identify outliers as they come up. The result is not only greater integrity, but also greater efficiency in our use of resources, courtesy of avoiding unnecessary detours and distractions. Everyone is "rowing in the same direction." Efforts are accelerated rather than diluted. And as business consultant Patrick Lencioni notes, "If you could get all the people in the organization rowing in the same direction, you could dominate any industry, in any market, against any competition, at any time."[49]

Which brings us back to impact. When you boil it down, do these reasons justify an investment in collaborative strategy development, particular in the absence of a clear link to results?

Despite significant shortcomings in strategic planning efforts and a shortage of robust, publicly accessible documentation, preliminary indications do show a defensible connection between planning and performance. For instance, a recent longitudinal study on the link between strategic planning and homelessness across multiple agencies indicated that beds for the homeless increased with greater diversity of participation in the planning process and the resulting richer plan designs.[50] Jordan Tama's public sector strategy research in the US showed that strategic planning "can help leaders and organizations make good decisions, operate more effectively and efficiently, focus on and institutionalize priorities, prepare for contingencies and crises, innovate, provide personnel with a sense of purpose, and serve the public well."[51] Increased stakeholder involvement has been proven to have positive effects on organizational performance.[52]

Leadership in strategic planning also strengthens the mediating factors that link plans with organizational results. A compelling strategy both attracts and deploys resources — funders want to invest in organizations that are focused and collaborative. Your organization optimizes the resources it needs to make the impact it exists to make, by having clear expectations and *sightlines* toward success. You attract and retain talent, because top people want to be associated with organizations that know what they want and are going after it. That's what's at stake.

Besides, think of the alternatives...

I often learn something best by considering what life would be like if that new thing were *not* true. So, in this case, what might be the consequences of having no plan, or even one developed in isolation rather than collaboratively? You might end up with exactly the opposite of the benefits listed above.

More specifically, you could expect to encounter some combination of the following:

Assumptions	If people don't understand how or why decisions were made, they fill in the blanks with their own story, which they soon believe to be true.
Disengagement	Without buy-in, you might have compliance but you won't have commitment.
Distractions	When decisions seem random, people's attention is diverted away from their work and toward curiosity (or resentment) about where these new priorities came from. Energy is scattered and focus is diluted.

Inertia
Without a fresh strategy, you risk perpetuating or even defending ways of working that are no longer serving you well.

Irrelevance
In the absence of a strategy informed by stakeholder engagement, your priorities may be disconnected from your market because you haven't solicited the wisdom of those you serve or serve alongside.

Meaninglessness
Your work risks becoming disconnected from its purpose or intended impact when that alignment is not explicitly checked.

Misunderstanding
Without thorough reconnaissance built through engaging your stakeholders and other environmental scanning activities, you risk making decisions in the absence of full information.

Could you smash out a plan over the weekend and hand it out on Monday morning? Sure you could. But it wouldn't stick. Investing time in development upfront yields returns in buy-in at the back end. As the saying goes, "go slow to go fast." Or as Simon Sinek puts it, "It's better to go slow in the right direction than to go fast in the wrong direction."

WHEN

Getting your timing right and setting
expectations about length and pace

When

PLAN? NOW?

I hesitate even to write the word "unprecedented", but these times will be studied in history class by our children and grandchildren, along with the world wars and the civil rights movement. When I first wrote this paragraph, it was day 26 of COVID-19 cocooning at home, and we'd already been radically disrupted and shaken to our core. Today, I've lost count. The shock is wearing off, but the ride isn't over yet. By the time you read this, our world will have changed again and again. The oxymoron of constant uncertainty characterizes our times.

Is it even possible to think about planning at a time like this, when our previous plans seem irrelevant, people are distracted and exhausted, and our ability to predict the future with any certainty seems non-existent?

We could never have planned for this. Can we plan during it?

I think we have to, for at least a baker's dozen reasons:

1. **Strategy is about making choices.** As Peter Drucker said, "the key to strategy is omission."[53] People are craving decisive leadership as a counterbalance to widespread uncertainty. Even, or perhaps especially, in times of disruptive change, we leaders have choices to make. These choices are primarily about where to put our attention and where not to. Given you are making choices every day, having a strategy in place lets you make them with intentionality and clear reference points.

2. **Strategy will spur you into action.** To develop a series of action steps against a timeline is to create a lever that will help you overcome inertia or the paralysis of being overwhelmed. Even if those action steps prove to be "the wrong ones," any sailor or

athletic coach will tell you that it is easier to change direction while you are moving than when you are stationary. As noted in an anecdote made famous by sense-making scholar Karl Weick, "any map will do."[54]

3. **You will be and feel less reactive.** Having a plan puts you on the front foot, ready for whatever comes — even if that future doesn't match your initial expectations. The sense of agency that accompanies having a plan is a calming and motivating force.

4. **Clear strategy gives you a competitive advantage.** Done well, a strategy sets you apart. As A. G. Lafley and Roger Martin write in *Playing to Win,* "Not only is strategy possible in times of tumultuous change, but it can be a competitive advantage and a source of significant value creation."[55] As Roger Rumelt expresses in *Good Strategy/Bad Strategy:* no one has an advantage at everything — press in where you have it, sidestep where you don't.[56] Strategic planning during a time of crisis is an opportunity to lean in.

5. **Strong strategy attracts resources.** Investors want to back people with a compelling vision and a plan for achieving it. Too many organizations spend their time whining about not having enough money instead of figuring out how they'd spend it if they did.

6. **The journey matters.** The co-creation of strategy with your team is a learning process that builds understanding, cohesion, and buy-in. The power of a shared experience and a co-created product is no less in times of turbulence than in times of stability.

7. **You need a coach when the game is on the line.** Football coach Tom Landry famously said, "A coach is someone who tells you what you don't want to hear, who has you see what you don't want to see, so you can be who you have always known you could be." To the extent that you draw on trusted advisors to help your organization develop strategy, the value of those thinking partners' perspectives is particularly high in unpredictable times where our past experiences are not faithful reference points for the future.

8. **Turbulence amplifies existing issues.** It's likely that the problems you are experiencing have accelerated in their pace or

urgency, but not in their kind. Strategy development now may help you to address issues that you needed to address all along, but with more acuity.

9. **We need simplification.** The complexity of strategic interactions requires a set of simplifying strategies to guide decisions. This is true in chess, in sports, and in business.[57] Although we must be wary of over-simplification, our brains need reliable ways to manage complexity and uncertainty.

10. **This will end, and things will re-stabilize.** It's likely your mission hasn't changed. Your "why" stays true even as your "how" is shifting. You are therefore wise to give deliberate thought to how to leverage that new "how" without losing sight of your "why." That's what strategic planning is all about. Develop some clarity now, and when the shape of the new normal begins to emerge, you will already have built momentum toward progress markers that are meaningful to you.

11. **Things are never not changing.** Are we really going to abandon planning until our context becomes more stable and certain? That time may never come. As Roger Martin muses, "If the future is too unpredictable and volatile to make strategic choices, what would lead a manager to believe that it will become significantly less so?"[58] We are better off learning to keep on looking down the long road even when it's bumpy than waiting for it to smooth out.

12. **Your past plan is in the past.** The world has changed too profoundly for you to carry on with business as usual. If you thought this was a year to dust off or tweak your old plan, it isn't. Going back to the way things were is not a viable option, so the relevance of your old plan (if you had one) in the new world is likely very low.

13. **Your crystal ball has always been broken.** Although it seems particularly difficult to predict the future with any accuracy right now, the truth is it always was. Strategic planning has never been about being clairvoyant. As strategy scholar Dr. Max Mckeown notes, "Since the future is uncertain, all your decisions will have an uncertain outcome. But because you're trying to shape the

future, you still need to decide."[59] Strategizing is about being insightful and intentional, disciplined and responsive. Those skills are futureproof.

So, let's continue to plan. Explicitly, deliberately, and collaboratively.

Planning that is done together, out loud, and on purpose is never wasted in terms of its process nor its product. But we do need to do it differently, in terms of pace and time horizon. We need to up our cadence and shorten our increments.

PLANNING HORIZONS

Five years used to be the accepted strategic planning rhythm. This stemmed from an implicit expectation that the future was stable and predictable over time. (That seems like naivety or hubris through today's lens, doesn't it?) It also reflected the pragmatism of good stewardship. Because fulsome strategic planning takes time to do and even longer to implement, people wanted more breathing space in their planning cycles. Five years allowed for a better return on investment than a shorter cycle would, especially if it took the first half-year to develop the plan in the first place. In recent years, that timeframe has shortened to three years as the pace of life accelerated and people became less confident in their ability to predict the future. Now, I'm seeing detailed plans on timelines as short as a year, or sometimes even a quarter.

But those compressed plans are situated within a longer sightline of perhaps five or ten years — not so much out of a desire to plan for longer as to cast visions that are shorter. Vision statements used to be seen as timeless, never-to-be-achieved aspirational declarations. Now, I see vision statements being replaced by credos, identity statements, or manifestos that are time-bound and read in the present tense. Purposeful but pragmatic. I suspect the days of lofty visions with timeframes equal to "forever" or "never" are numbered.

Concurrently, I see the planning cadence radically speeding up. Contexts are complex and rapidly changing, and they're being disrupted in unfore-seeable ways. Relevance is of critical concern to organizations not just once in a generation but even once per year. So strategies are not only shorter, but are being developed more often. And if strategies are being developed annually or every eighteen months, it doesn't make sense to take six to twelve months to do so.

PRO TIP

Make sure that your investment in the planning exercise is roughly proportional to the length of the plan. But factor in the culture-building benefit of collaborative planning when you're doing your math.

People are planning in shorter increments while looking down a longer road. They're lifting their gaze to make sure their short-term plans are taking them in the direction they want to go, but faster.

When you ride a bicycle or a motorcycle, you are more likely to stay upright if your eyes are up and forward. Your body will respond more nimbly when your gaze is fixed on the horizon. Look at the road immediately in front of you, and you're more apt to topple. The same is true for today's leaders. Twists and turns — maybe even dramatic climbs and pitches — are inevitable. Keep your eyes up and forward.

Savvy up

It is useful to think about which of your current undertakings are likely to persist in the short and the longer term, and which will need to be let go. Dr. Jason Fox would say the continuing ones are the areas where you need to "savvy up,"[60] not just blindly continue. Strategic planning is about making decisions after all, and the word "decide" means to cut off or kill other options. When it comes to timing, it helps to consider not only which elements will be cut off, but how quickly, and which other ones might be needed temporarily to achieve longer-term aims. Still other activities will continue throughout the life of your plan.

PRO TIP

Consider starting your planning process with what you'll stop doing. It's a hard question, but its answer will free up capacity to take on new things, or even just to consider them.

In your planning conversations, it helps to give some vocabulary to each of the regions in the diagram on the following page ("Is this 'now' thing going to last or not last?" "Is this something that's going to overlap into the 'now' and the 'after'?" "Is this something we're going to be letting go or something we're going to be starting up?") so that you have a sense of both continuity and newness, along with a sense of things scaling down or stopping altogether. In the COVID-19 era in which I write, these three circles might be labelled "Before," "Now," and "After".

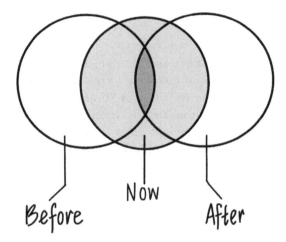

Another way of depicting this shared sense of timing is using a visual shaped like an infinity loop, similar to the approach to Ecocycle Planning described in *The Surprising Powers of Liberating Structures*.[61] It shows ideas at all stages: those that are in their early incubation phase, those that are growing, others that are maturing, and some that are in fact dying, making space for the birth and incubation of new initiatives. Looking at your planning as a cycle of birth, life, maturity, death, and renewal is actually more helpful than seeing it on a linear, multi-year pathway. It can help you visualize when to invest and lean in, and when to loosen your grip and let go.

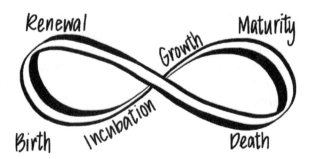

HOW LONG WILL PLANNING TAKE?

I often get asked how long a strategic planning process will take. In some ways this is like asking how long is a piece of string!

In my experience, there's a chunk of the planning process that stays roughly the same each time, and is therefore somewhat predictable in its length. It's the pieces that get added on at each end that primarily determine the overall length of the process. It tends to work like this:

The core of the planning process — developing goals, objectives, activities, rough measurements — usually takes roughly 10 to 14 hours of collaborative time if it is facilitated well. That number can grow if you run into particularly sticky issues with the group that result in a deep lack of consensus, and/or if decision rights have not been clarified. But roughly speaking, if I can get two days of total work time with a group in a room, we can get that core planning done.

Environmental scanning activities such as stakeholder engagement and research can add to that timeline at the front end. Some organizations choose not to do extensive stakeholder engagement every time, whereas others consider the team-building and goodwill-building benefit of strategic planning to be well worth the investment every time.

Conversations about the organization's identity statements, depending on whether you are in a "major" or "minor" planning cycle, also lengthen the project. I find that organizations need to do a fulsome overhaul about every third planning cycle — perhaps once a decade — where they take a hard look at their reason for being. They reconsider their mission, their vision, and maybe their governance structure. These elements should outlast your strategies, so strategic planning cycles of perhaps three years can be nested inside of that decade, like chapters in a longer story. So it's important to understand whether you're in a minor cycle or a major cycle (I call this an "overhaul" or "tweak"), as that will affect the time and effort you invest in the process.

No
change   Tweak   Evolution   Overhaul

The other end of the planning cycle — implementation planning — can be slow or quick as well. Some organizations consider the strategic planning process to have been completed when broad targets are ready to be passed off to departmental managers for implementation planning to occur. For others, that detailed operational planning that cascades through the organization is in fact part of the strategic planning process itself.

The length of the planning process also depends on the availability of those involved. This is true for all busy people, but especially for volunteers who sit on social benefit boards. The timing is less dependent on the components of the process itself than on the willingness of the players to make themselves available to do the work.

PRO TIP

Design your process with people's availability in mind. If you're working in a rural context, don't expect folks to give input into your planning process right at harvest season. Don't ask seniors to drive in a snowstorm. Avoid scheduling meetings with parents of young children during afternoon naps or school pick-up time. A bit of anticipation, empathy, and courtesy will increase your engagement rates.

Gone are the days when a board could book a strategic planning retreat and come home strategic plan in hand. I say that for a couple of reasons. First, because corporate offsites tend to be rarer than they used to be, as companies just don't want to invest the time or money. And second, because I think it's important to manage expectations. A fulsome strategic plan cannot be built in one day. We can generate the core components — the key "ingredients" — but now is not the time to be finalizing the wording. That's best left to a separate team with fresh eyes. (And word-smithing as a group is awful anyway!)

Moreover, people's brains need percolation time. My preference is to have shorter, more frequent meetings rather than one long retreat. I do like to have a core workshop in the middle of the process, because being away together has all kinds of other team-building benefits, but for planning benefits, if you can free people from distraction, I find that a series of three-hour meetings ends up being much more productive than marathon sessions at a retreat.

At the end of the day, I find that a strategic plan usually takes somewhere between six weeks and six months to develop. I worked with one organization that decided to take a full year, though they worked on many things at once, including a full organizational theory of change, a new organizational structure, and governance training with their board.

Roughly four months is more common.

Resolving dilemmas related to staff and board roles, having too many voices or too few, and other tricky considerations about whose job strategy making really is

Who

WHO SHOULD DO THE PLANNING?

As with the other parts of this process, the decision as to who should be involved in the planning process is yours to make. There is no single right answer, but this section will help you think about how to decide.

Most importantly, be clear where decision rights lie. Decide and communicate, clearly and often, who gets to make decisions at which points in the process, including whose job is it to set strategy, who will give input into possible strategic options, who implements the strategy, who will measure the achievement against it, and to whom those results will be reported. An orientation toward transparent, defensible, robust decision-making processes will lead to deliverables that share those same characteristics.

Many non-profits have governance boards — boards that are moving toward a policy/governance model and away from operations. In these cases, strategy falls within the board's portfolio of responsibility. If yours is a more operational board, strategy likely still falls to you, as it is an appropriate board role, and there's no one else to do it! In transitioning toward becoming a governance board, Directors sometimes lose their sense of purpose and feel disconnected from the mission that got them excited about being involved with the organization in the first place. Strategic planning provides them with an opportunity to engage legit-imately, to make a direct contribution to something important and useful for the organization. I would not recommend taking that away from them. Strategic planning can be a powerful tool for board engagement.

Yet there are many boards that fully recognize strategic planning as their responsibility, but exercise that responsibility by simply knowing with confidence that it's being handled competently by someone else. Sometimes there is a gap between the board's responsibility for strategy planning and their actual expertise. They may not have the necessary time, information, or skills to be able to do it well. You don't want your hands tied by requiring your directors to do something for which they are ill-equipped. The time that even a highly committed board member spends thinking about the organization may only be ten percent or even one percent of the time spent by that organization's senior leaders. The latter are therefore well positioned to be active in strategy making.

As Cowley and Domb assert, "the plans are best made by the doers."[62] When considering which staff inside your organization should be involved, the choice is not only about positions in the organizational hierarchy. It is worth considering that not everyone is equally interested in or gifted at this kind of work. Who lives your values, instinctively believes deeply in your organization's mission, and has already thought about what your organization needs to look like in the future because they just can't help themselves? These are the people you want on your strategy team. You need to balance the tension between being inclusive and being selective so as to build on evident strengths.

In their study of cognitive styles and public sector planning, Bert George and colleagues found that processing styles of participants affect planning outcomes. They divided participants into "creators, knowers and planners," and, perhaps unexpectedly, discovered that creators — people who have a high tolerance for ambiguity — were most likely to see strategic plans as both useful and easy to use.[63] Who do you have that is wired to do this kind of creative work, who can combine big-picture thinking with practicality, all in a context of uncertainty? This is their time to shine. And they may not be who you think.

PRO TIP

Consider involving unusual collaborators in your planning process. After all, if the people around your planning table created and benefit from your current working arrangements, how likely are they to be the ones to suggest radically changing it?

Many of my clients have established a Strategic Planning Steering Committee comprising representatives of their board and senior staff. Such a team strikes a useful balance between those who will be responsible for the implementation of the plan and those who can give it governance insight or more of an insider/outsider perspective. For some, it is also useful to include people with recent frontline exposure. The scope of work of this committee, including any limits on its ability to make decisions or recommendations, should be made explicit from the outset. So too should the opportunities for wider participation at key moments in the process.

I have participated in many planning workshops where the conversations were enriched by the presence of a sharp CEO of a partner organization, a retired board member, an academic with expertise in a relevant field, and/or client representatives. Eliciting this broad advice is especially possible and fruitful in the community sector, where guarding competitive advantage and proprietary knowledge are less critical. But I would welcome private sector readers to bravely consider the benefits of something similar.

When seeking out opportunities for staff involvement in the planning process, consider the size of your staff and the kinds of expertise they will contribute to the eventual product. I find that ideation (think brainstorming), checking decisions, and mapping out rollout implications are usually great opportunities for wider input. Framing the project and making key decisions along the way (at least provisionally) are usually more manageably undertaken by a smaller group. Whenever you involve new people in the planning process, it's important to set expectations, since participation and clear process build buy-in. For example, be clear if you are asking them for ideas, advice, or to make a decision.

Another critical consideration is how you plan to address issues of justice, diversity, equity, and inclusion. The composition of your planning team and the design of your engagement are two places of many where you can ensure your process is reflective of the diversity of the communities you serve. How are the perspectives of people with lived experience of the issues you address being incorporated in your strategy making?

PRO TIP

Sometimes I encounter concern that more junior or frontline staff will be less able to keep the interests of the whole organization in mind if involved in strategy making conversations. In my experience, if the expectations are framed carefully, this fear is usually unfounded. They bring useful perspectives, and the professional growth they experience by being involved increases their allegiance and value to the company.

An additional consideration is whether you undertake the strategic planning process with the support of an outside consultant or facilitator, or will it be handled internally? This choice entails a number of considerations, but here are the five I think are most critical.

Do you realistically have:

- the internal *skills* in strategy development and facilitation to lead this process?
- the *time* to manage and implement this project at the right pace? Will it gain momentum and get the attention it needs, given your current capacity?

- the *neutrality* of an outside voice? Perceived objectivity can be critical, including for change management.

- the *credibility* to communicate with candor and catalyze change?

- the *funds* to hire an outsider? (Don't make the mistake of thinking that handling the project internally is "free" or faster...)

If you are considering enlisting in an outside consulting team, be clear about the specific support that team would be bringing to your organization, from occasional advice to facilitation of key workshops to full project design and management.

Dr. Max Mckeown affirms the importance of investing in expert facilitation, since the future of your business should be valuable to you.[64] Yet it's important to understand that hiring an outside person to support your strategic planning work does not mean divesting yourself of the task. As previously mentioned, strategic planning requires a series of decisions, and those decisions cannot be delegated to an outsider. Leaders need to lead. Your external facilitator can shepherd you through a process to help your Steering Committee consider and advise on those decisions, but ultimately they are yours to make. It's important that the content, language, and energy of the plan be yours.

You want to be careful not to fall into the trap of outsourcing a sense of ownership of the plan. This can happen quite insidiously. Even though your people have likely been involved in workshopping the plan's components, the writing of it is a time-consuming task that is often delegated, at least in draft form, to the outside consulting team. The risk here, of course, is that the written product may not sound like your voice or feel like it carries your organization's personality. It may not reflect the emphases or even intentions that were voiced internally. There are many points in the process where it's possible for the plan to shift from being your plan to being the consultant's plan — or, more accurately, a consultant report with a series of recommendations for your consideration, rather than a deliverable that is in fact yours and ready to be rolled out. Determining who is responsible for actually writing the plan is thus very important. As Wolf and Floyd's research found, "The understanding of and commitment to strategy by organizational members are both influenced by the way plans are designed and presented."[65]

*Illuminating the pathways to your deliverables,
including the decisions you need to make and
activities you can use to get there*

Ways

The details in this section might be the reason you picked up this book. ("I have a strategic plan to get done and have no idea where to start!") It might also be the one you skim or skip ("I'm hiring an outside expert to navigate this planning process and am banking on her having read this section!") Either way, here is where we get out of the clouds and down to the nitty gritty.

I've already noted that there are lots of ways to develop a solid strategic plan. I am outlining the steps I often follow. It's an approach, but it's not an iron-clad model. You might be surprised to learn that the strategic planning literature is scant on comprehensive models. A search of strategic planning models most often yields individual tools (such as a SWOT or PEST analysis) that may be useful at one stage of planning, but explain little about where in the process they fit, or what other steps are needed on either side in order to get to a finished product.

Bill Staples' *Transformational Strategy*[66] and Michael Wilkinson's *The Executive Guide to Facilitating Strategy*[67] are two notable exceptions to the above rule, but they both risk being too prescriptive about how to carry out planning, inferring that it follows identical steps every time. Suggesting there is one best way feels too rigid and scripted. On the other hand, by avoiding any prescription at all you run the risk of describing too many possibilities and losing the reader in the complexity of hypothetical scenarios. As one client recently said to me, "Just tell me how to do this!" So where does the balance come from?

I have decided to frame the "how" in terms of the *decision* you need to make at each step, the *deliverable* you're going after, the *key question* you need to answer, and a *suggested activity* to get there. By breaking it down in this way you should be able to have a clear framework yet be able to fill it with your own scenarios. The decisions reflect the strategic choices that are on the table as you go along. The deliverables are the outputs generated by each step. You can think of them as the headings for the table of contents if you were to draft a detailed final report of your strategic planning process. The key question can focus your attention during each step. I offer one or more suggested methodologies or facilitated activities for answering each question and generating the associated deliverable. These elements zoom in at quite a granular level and will be particularly useful for people thinking about the details of how to run planning meetings. If that's not you, feel free to jump to the next step. Once you are prepared to answer the key question thoroughly and well, it's time to move on.

We'll look at a wide range of deliverables, but realize that your organization may not need every deliverable, every time. Likewise, you may approach the steps differently to how they are laid out here. Some steps might happen concurrently; others might be combined. Some may generate a distinct product; others will be incorporated into your eventual planning report without ever standing alone. The activities might not suit your group in every case. Remember what I said, that a strategic plan is yours and is supposed to serve you. Ditto for the process to get to it. You choose what makes sense. I hope to give you enough details to equip you to make those choices, without overwhelming you with possibilities.

Strategic planning is not something most people do very often. It's a multi-step process that can be complex and messy. Organizations often lack the resources or capacity to do it well.[68] While the previous sections underscored the importance of making that investment, this section will outline in greater detail specifically what's required.

"In the word question, there's a beautiful word — quest. I love that word."

॰— Elie Wiesel —॰

Catalytic Questions

I'm excited for us to get into the real work of strategy making, and as a primer, let me mention the power of curiosity. In his book *Questions Are the Answer*, Hal Gregerson talks about the power of catalytic questions.[69] In chemistry, a catalyst knocks down barriers and channels energy into more productive pathways. Really great questions can do the same thing. They have a curious power to unlock insights and behaviour change. Einstein is famous for having encouraged people never to lose their "holy curiosity." In *The Power of Onlyness*, Nilofer Merchant asserts that questions "challenge the invisible walls that frame an idea."[70] As Chip Conley suggests, innocent questions fuel innovation.[71] Carry this attitude through **the six A's of strategy making** and you'll find you get a lot more out of your team and your time.

The questions don't just define your outcomes, but also you yourself. Great leaders ask great questions. In *A More Beautiful Question*, Warren Berger suggests that brilliant changemakers throughout history have been exceptionally good at asking questions. He says "the corner office is for the askers."[72] Amanda Lang argues that the willingness to keep asking questions is more important to successful innovation than huge originality is.[73] Tim Ferriss puts it another way, advocating for asking "the right dumb question."[74] Edgar Schein suggests timing your questions carefully, asking them "… at the right time, when the group is ready to see the problem for themselves."[75]

Leaders also play a critical role in creating space for other people's questioning. John Wooden is famous for having said, "It's what you learn after you know it all that counts." Hal Gregersen refers to "questioning capital," whereby people earn the right, either through their position or their reputation, to ask questions and be heard.[76] In *Humble Inquiry*, Edgar Schein asserts that those who are higher in the organizational pecking order must take responsibility for enabling their subordinates to safely express their curiosity.[77] Leaders can bestow that questioning capital on others.

Finally, asking questions is not just about finding things out. In collaborative strategy development, it is easy to latch onto particular ideas too soon. Good questions allow us to explore and be open to a wider range of solutions. As Richard Rumelt asserts, we are wise to stay curious rather than making and justifying our choices too early in the game.[78]

THE SIX A'S OF STRATEGY MAKING

It's time for the deep work! My approach to strategy making is based on a six-step model: Anticipate, Attune, Align, Assess, Adapt, and Archive. We're going to work through this model in some detail, so that you can build a clear sightline to the strategic outcomes of your organisation.

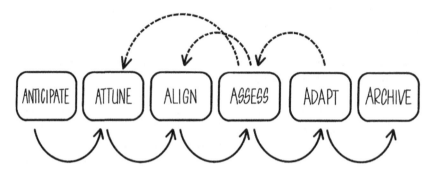

Step one is to **anticipate** what might be required. Following that,

Step two is to become intentionally **attuned** to your environment.

Step three, you **align** your organization's plans with the relevant features of that environment.

Step four is to **assess** how well your draft plan matches your aspirations for it.

Step five, you **adapt** your deployment of resources to achieve that alignment.

Step six, is maintaining an **archive** to bolster organizational memory by documenting what you did to get there and why.

The deliverables, key questions, and activities nested within each of the six phases are summarized in the following tables.

ANTICIPATE

DELIVERABLE	DECISION	KEY QUESTION	HOW TO
1. Definition of "done"	What "finished" looks like	What will we have generated, experienced, and learned by the end of this project?	Share expectations
2. Process design	Extent of engagement	Who will be involved, when, why, and how?	Engagement mapping

ATTUNE

DELIVERABLE	DECISION	KEY QUESTION	HOW TO
3. Contextual analysis	Whom/What to listen to	What are the key trends happening around us that are critically relevant to our plan?	Trends research and stakeholder engagement
4. Identity statements	Extent to which these statements will shape the plan or be shaped by it	What impact do we exist to have in the world?	Know your "why"
5. Theory of change	What you believe about how change happens	How do we understand the links between our actions and the changes we most want to influence?	Working hypotheses

DELIVERABLE	DECISION	KEY QUESTION	HOW TO
6. Positioning	Relevance	Given what's going on, who we are, and what we do, what must we pay attention to and become known for in this planning cycle?	And therefore...
7. Strategic pillars	Scaffolding for the strategy	What are the "big buckets" of work that will structure our strategy?	Big buckets
8. Goals	What to pursue	What do you want to be different at the end of this planning cycle compared to what is true now?	Attention to achieve intention
9. Objectives	How we are going to get this done	What are the smaller projects that will lead to the achievement of our larger goal?	Building blocks
10. Performance standards	How to measure performance	What level of progress deserves a gold star?	Know your win
11. Key activities	Where to start	What do we most need to get busy doing?	Get 'er done

ASSESS

DELIVERABLE	DECISION	KEY QUESTION	HOW TO
12. Quality check	Whether we're "done" enough to proceed	Is this a good strategy?	Check-ins

DELIVERABLE	DECISION	KEY QUESTION	HOW TO
13. Capacity analysis	What it will take to execute this strategy	Do we have what it takes?	What it will require
14. Implementation plan	How to get 'er done	Specifically, who's doing what when?	Once again, define "done"
15. Execution systems	How to stick with it	What habits do we need to develop?	Stacking
16. Monitoring plan	How to know whether the strategy is happening and working	How are we doing and how do we know?	Systematically flexible

DELIVERABLE	DECISION	KEY QUESTION	HOW TO
17. Organizational memory	How to capture the strategy-making process for future reference	What did we decide and why?	Methodology Rationale Reflections

We'll now unpack each element of the 6A's table in greater detail so that you can bring it to life in your own organizational context.

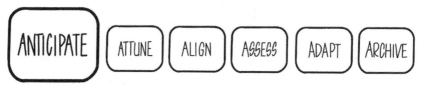

- Definition of "done"
- Process design

DEFINITION OF DONE

DELIVERABLE

A provisional statement describing the finished package.

In my work lately, this package often includes a two-page summary, with one page designed for external viewing and the more detailed version intended as an internal reminder of the highlights of the strategy; a slide deck; and a 12- to 15-page report that describes the methodology followed and brief rationale for key decisions. That longer report might sit untouched on a shelf much of the time, but it's an important tool for maintaining organizational memory, as we'll see in **Archive.**

DECISION

What "finished" looks like.

Do you have a picture in your head of what your plan will look like when it's done?

I don't mean what will it say, but what will you have generated and for whom? A report? An infographic? A slide deck? A two-pager? A mural? Your answer might be several of these, or none of them. Which pieces will be inward facing and which will be designed for external audiences? In addition to what you will have physically generated, this is also the time to consider your desired experiential outcomes. What do you want participants to have felt or learned? You may not even be completely sure at the outset, but it does help to have a shared understanding with your full project team as to what "finished" and "successful" is likely to look like. Begin with the end in mind.[79]

KEY QUESTION

What will we have generated, experienced, and learned by the end of this project?

———

HOW TO

Share expectations.

This is a fairly straightforward first step that involves a conversation with the key people leading the project. Your strategic plan needs to be useful to you, so consider what will actually get used. Ask the following questions and pay attention to the extent of agreement around the table:

- What do we need the plan to be or do for us?
- What time horizon do we want the plan to cover?
- Who are the key audiences?
- What formats would those audiences be most likely to use?
- Do we imagine creating more than one version for different audiences?

Agree on your intended final products, then hold them loosely. This is an intention, not a fixed script, but it is a necessary starting point.

WHAT DOES "DONE" LOOK LIKE?

This diagram shows you an outline of the product you will end up with, once you have completed your strategic plan.

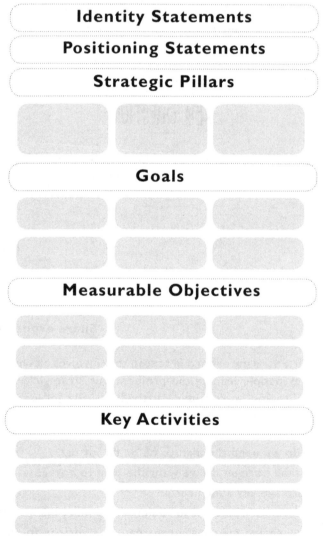

Identity Statements

Positioning Statements

Strategic Pillars

Goals

Measurable Objectives

Key Activities

Strategic Plan Outline

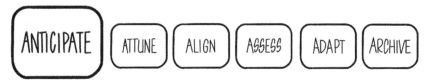

- Definition of "done"
- Process design

PROCESS DESIGN

DELIVERABLE

A visual project plan structured along a timeline.

This is a road map to show you key milestones along the timeline. It will also indicate who will be involved, and to what extent, at each phase of the project.

DECISION

Extent of engagement.

Before you make decisions about the content of your strategic plan, you need to confirm the process by which you intend to develop it.

I have already made the case for planning collaboratively as a starting point. A fulsome treatment of stakeholder engagement planning, while beyond the scope of this section, is thoroughly handled elsewhere.[80]

For now, it is sufficient to plot out a high-level process map to support communication, recruitment of participants, and project management.

KEY QUESTION

Who will be involved, when, why, and how?

———

HOW TO

———

Engagement mapping.

To develop your engagement map, I recommend zooming out, in, and back out again.

The first step is to map out the main phases of your process along a timeline, which is best achieved from a broad, "zoomed out" perspective. You could use the six A's with their associated deliverables as a starting point, or develop stages of your own. Make it visual.

Now   Done

Next, I suggest zooming in to work out specifically who you'd like to involve, to what extent, when, and how.

The first two decisions to make in designing that engagement are:

1. Who has the information you need?
2. How extensive do you want stakeholder engagement to be?

These are tricky questions, and their answers are related. Part of the wisdom of stakeholder engagement design is in discerning when enough is enough, and your budget might be the deciding factor. There are always more people you could talk to, but eventually you will reach a saturation point when you are hearing very little new information, or you have invested what you consider to be a sufficient amount in this phase, proportional to the rest of the project. The value of any new input you receive should be aligned with your investment to gather and analyze it. You want to optimize your design in service of the purposes you're trying to achieve.

POWER / INTEREST GRID

INFLUENCE
ON DECISION

IMPACTED
BY DECISION

Engagement planning can be done by the leader, the steering team, or a broader group. There are many stakeholder mapping tools and processes available. For instance, a tool such as the one shown here can be helpful in identifying and locating key stakeholders. (Filling it in can also be useful in surfacing differences of opinion amongst participants as to where stakeholders belong on this map!) The idea is to identify the people who have power to influence the success of your plan and interest in being involved based on the degree to which they are impacted by the decision.[81]

Unfortunately, I find that mapping tools tend to be too generic to be useful if not translated into a more detailed plan. The tendency is for stakeholders to be identified too generally. For instance, if your team notes "funders" or "media" or "government" as being important, you'll still leave the meeting not knowing who to call. On the other end of the spectrum, people may work very specifically, listing individual names, but often these names are not accompanied by any explicit rationale as to why they ought to be involved. I therefore translate the stakeholder mapping tool into a planning template like the one shown later in this section. If you find it challenging to fill it in at this early stage, not to worry — you can add detail as the project goes along.

This is a good time to confirm the "why" behind the involvement of each stakeholder group. This "why" has three parts:

1. Why that organization or stakeholder group?
2. Who from within that group will we access and why?
3. What role are we asking them to play?

In turn, their role will determine two things:

- The *timing of their involvement*. (If you are asking for ideas, for example, that input should come earlier than if you are inviting people to choose amongst options or set priorities from a list of necessary actions.)

- The *extent of their influence* on the final decision(s) being made. (More on collaborative decision making later, but for now it comes down to this: Are you asking people to give input into a decision, or to make it?)[82]

Once the "who" and "why" of the engagement plan is settled, you can turn your attention to the "how" for the various stages of your process. There are a number of trade-offs inherent in this key design question. In particular, you must strike a balance between reach and depth. A key initial filtering question is: "Is it more important for us to reach lots of people, or to reach deep understanding with a few people?" Most processes cannot afford to do both. Your answer will help to narrow down the range of engagement tools you might consider.

A second filtering question is: "Will this engagement moment happen synchronously (meaning participants engage at the same time as each other), or asynchronously (meaning participants can engage when and as they want to)?" Generally speaking, asynchronous tools extend reach and affordability, whereas synchronous tools (live virtual, or in-person when available) are better at deepening understanding, capturing nuance, and being adaptive.

Answering these two filtering questions will help you narrow down the range of tools available to you at each stage, as summarized on the next page.

Stakeholder Engagement Planning Template

Who/Why

Stakeholder group	Specifically who	Why involve them

What/Why

What to ask them	Why	Access/ location

How/Where/When

Timing in the project	Which tool/medium	Who makes contact

A quick word on selecting methodologies: Surveys are static but inexpensive and give you wide reach, whereas conversational methods give you a smaller sample size but are more flexible and nuanced.

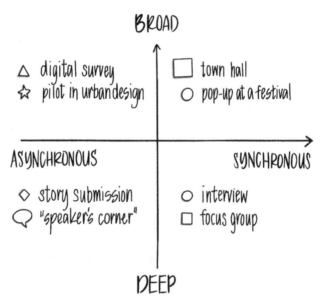

Once you have selected your engagement opportunities and decided upon appropriate methods for each, you can then return to your project timeline and insert more detail as to where key engagement milestones will occur.

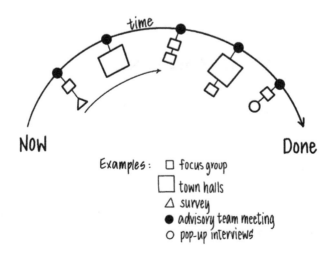

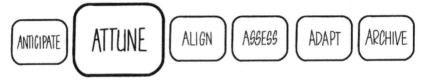

- Contextual analysis
- Identity statements
- Theory of Change

The **Attune** phase is about paying attention to what is going on around you. It is about developing what I call your "reconnaissance capacity," which allows you to receive the intelligence you need in order to plan.

The word "attune" is apt. My son is a cellist. As he learned his instrument, he was coached to "listen for the ringers." Those were the notes where the vibration of the strings was at its richest because his fingers were in exactly the right place, exerting the right amount of pressure at the right time. It is a skill learned in part through muscle memory but mostly by training the ear to recognize when the pitch is exactly right. Tuning your ear to the frequencies you most need to hear is what this phase of planning is all about.

CONTEXTUAL ANALYSIS

DELIVERABLE

A briefing document summarizing what you have learned from your analysis of context.

I would suggest capturing trend information in one of three ways, one is to summarize the findings of this step into a table like so:

Trend/Data	"So what" for us in 5–10 years?

A second option is to structure your analysis by scale to create a summary that captures similar information, but organizes it by the level of "zoom" as shown below.

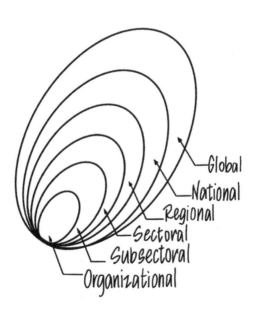

Another possibility is to write a more traditional briefing document summarizing what you've heard and learned thus far.

The choice depends on the level of detail or rigour you want to include in this step, and of course personal preference.

DECISION

What to listen to.

Once your internal design steps are complete, the first outward-facing step involves lifting your gaze from your day-to-day work and looking around. You may have heard this called an "environmental scan."

The key question I ask here is not simply, "What's happening in the wider world?" but "What's happening in the wider world that our organization must take into account as it plans?" and further, *"What does that trend mean for us?"* Your organization's environment is a socially constructed and mediated phenomenon — it is not sitting out there waiting to be discovered, nor is it homogeneous or static. This step is therefore about taking a snapshot and being selective about what details to highlight as relevant.

Environmental scanning involves holding a few things in tension. It is important to be rigorous and look for evidence, not just anecdotes. You want to think beyond your own sector into fields not typically associated directly with yours. Yet at the same time, it is important to be selective. Remember that your goal is to identify those trends that are critical to your organization right now, as it sets its path into the future. It is not to be the most accurate or comprehensive futurist or social commentator you can be. You therefore need to be good at anticipating the future without trying to be clairvoyant. Your job might be to connect potentially dissimilar things in unexpected ways. In that sense, it is a creative task, more than simple reportage. As Steve Jobs said, "Creativity is just connecting things."[83] You are also being a curator, choosing the cultural currents that are most relevant to you and letting the others drift by. This step therefore requires strategic insight, not just description.

As shown in the level of "zoom" figure on the previous page, your "environment" is not just outside of your organization, but includes it. The internal environment must also be taken into consideration. What did you learn from your last strategic planning process? Are you on the brink of a leadership change? Are you experiencing a period of rapid expansion? How unified is your team? Is there a challenge that has you stymied and is repeatedly inhibiting your progress? What is keeping you up at night? These reflective questions are key to understanding the context in which your strategy making occurs and to which it should respond. Usefully, leaders frequently look back on planning processes as having created the space they needed to have the conversations that led to their organization getting unstuck in many of these areas.

KEY QUESTION

What are the key trends happening around us that are critically relevant to our plan?

HOW TO

Trends research and stakeholder engagement.

It is time to refer back to the stakeholder engagement plan you developed in the previous step and execute the portions relevant to environmental scanning. Talk to the people who have access to the range of perspectives you need.

This step requires "big-picture thinking" of the highest order. It's one part of the process where your internal people may not be equipped, in terms of time or perspective, to paint the full picture you need. Then again, you may determine that, for the purposes of this exercise, they definitely do.

There is no one right way to do this. But it's easier to make a decision when you have a proposal to consider, so I will describe four options here that will help you customize your approach. The approach you choose will likely be some blend of the options described here. Each scenario has you asking people what trends your organization must take into account as it plans for the future. What differs is who casts the net, and how wide or deep they cast it.

1. Read up

There are smart people who make their living analyzing trends. Learn from them. Read the news. Read books by futurists,[84] then figure out what their assertions might mean for your work. Gather evidence to inform your conclusions.

2. Identify internal and external trends in-house

For this approach, you rely on your people "in the room." You invite your key people to come together and identify the trends the organization should take into account as it looks ahead. It is a conversation that may occur at the beginning of a strategic planning retreat, for example. This event would usually involve your leadership team and board of directors, or representatives thereof, working from the assumption that together they bring enough collective wisdom to answer the question adequately. The more diverse your leaders, the more likely this assumption will hold true. You may also choose to invite others to participate, to increase the breadth of perspectives. It may be useful to organize people's input into the levels shown previously, either as you gather it or afterwards.

3. Talk to your network

If you see benefit in moving beyond your internal team or published research, you could use this strategic planning task as an opportunity to set up telephone calls or coffee dates with key people in your network. Ask for their perspectives and advice. What are they noticing about your sector or where your organization is placed within it? They will likely be flattered you asked and open to helping even further. You may experience the Ben Franklin effect, where "the one that has once done you a kindness will be more ready to do you another, than [the one] whom you yourself have obliged."[85]

Most will provide you with thoughtful input. But do remember that the amount of time they'll spend thinking about your organization is a fraction of what you'll spend. Tailor your questions to reflect their actual expertise, because they'll likely willingly give you their opinions regardless of how well informed those opinions happen to be!

4. Ask for help

It is surprising to me in my work as a strategy consultant how openly people will talk to a perceived outsider, even when they are fully aware their feedback will make it back to the person or organization about whom they speak. Not with attribution, of course, but despite protection of anonymity never being fully guaranteed, people often seem to be willing to be a bit more candid with a third party. A third party is also willing to ask edgier questions since they are not directly implicated by the responses.

This is why a common approach to stakeholder engagement involves hiring an outside person to conduct surveys, interviews, or focus groups with key informants who can give your organization trusted advice. That input is then aggregated and fed back to your team in a report. You get the benefit of a fresh perspective on the input (and as I've said, that freshness may actually improve the quality of the input in the first place), and you don't have to scramble to find time to get these interviews done internally. You are, however, outsourcing the opportunity to strengthen direct relationships with your stakeholders, which may not be something you wish to delegate to someone who is only temporarily on the scene.

Be sure to choose a combination of methods that generate data in a quantity and format that you can actually process and use. It might be really fun and interactive to ask people to craft newspaper headlines from 2035, or to submit a video describing their vision for your organization, or to build a massive asset map out of sticky notes on the wall — but what will you do with what you get? Will you have time to analyze all that data coming to you in multiple formats? This is yet another situation where you should always begin with the end in mind.

There are lots of effective ways to do an environmental scan. Whichever tool you choose, be sure to link your strategic choices back to what you have learned.

Swatting at SWOT

A note about SWOT before we move on. Yes, you could use a SWOT (strengths, weaknesses, opportunities, threats) analysis here. But I wouldn't. Why? Because it seems like such a cliché to me — it's overdone. Also, the categories are not mutually exclusive. As Kieran Flanagan and Dan Gregory note in *Forever Skills*, "every Strength casts a shadow and every Weakness has an upside."[86] Worse, people confuse SWOT with strategic planning (I've had clients try to hire me explicitly to do a SWOT analysis thinking it's a strategy. Let's start with purpose, not method!). And perhaps more importantly, SWOT analyses don't actually tend to influence actual planning decisions. People obediently "fill in the SWOT boxes" then promptly forget about them and move on to whatever they intended to do anyway. The "so what" of SWOT is quickly lost. If you're still into it, go for it. Please just do it well. And if you're looking for a refreshed, more affirmative SWOT-like tool, SOAR[87] (strengths, opportunities, aspirations, results) might suit you better.

Identity Statements

Positioning Statements

Strategic Pillars

Goals

Measurable Objectives

Key Activities

Strategic Plan Outline: Identity

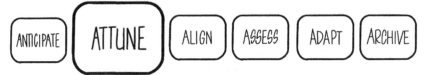

- Contextual analysis
- Identity statements
- Theory of Change

IDENTITY STATEMENTS

DELIVERABLE

A series of statements that describe what your organization exists to do, for whom, and why.

DECISION

The extent to which these statements will shape the plan or be shaped by it.

This next segment turns our attention to the "why" of the organization. And this may seem obvious, but in fact it's one of the moments in strategic planning that causes people to struggle most often, and you don't want to get bogged down near the start! Maybe it's difficult because organizational identity initially seems self-evident, but then in a room you discover that what might be apparent to you is not shared by the person next to you. "Common sense" is actually not that common! So it's really important to have explicit conversations about things that you might think are obvious. And in this case, that so-called obvious thing is the "why" of the organization.

This step gets us thinking about what would be lost if the organization did not exist. You can unpack this in terms of whom it serves, the needs it meets, the gaps it fills, the problems it solves, and the impact or results it's seeking to achieve. Perhaps the geography it covers or the core audience whose needs it meets.

The thinking here is on results and purpose, not so much on the activities or tactics that keep people busy each day. If you can develop a clear, shared image of why an organization exists, it will serve as your north star to make decisions later in the plan. A strategic plan, as we've said, is a useful tool for saying no to things, and one of the main reasons for saying no to a particular opportunity is that it is not well aligned with the core mission of the organization. Staying true to your core essence provides the sightline for the rest of the plan.

"Identity statements" are my category title for your organization's Mission, Vision, Values, Impact Statements... any combination of text that describes who you are, why you exist, and the impact you seek to make in the world. I have named them as such for two reasons:

1. I rather like the generic nature of the title. It helps people not get too stuck on "Is this our vision or our mission?" by instead simply asking, "What do you want to say about yourselves that describes your work at its core?"

2. I'm finding that some clients prefer to describe their core who/why/what in various ways that diverge from the traditional "Mission Vision Values" format. And that's fine. You describe your core identity in whatever ways make sense to you, serve your eventual strategic plan, and help you introduce yourself in an honest and meaning-ful way. One company has a "credo," another has a "manifesto." Several organizations I know simply introduce themselves by way of a descriptive paragraph entitled "Hi!" or "Who we really are" or "About us." As with your overall plan, your identity statements are yours to craft as you please.

The identity statements represent the pivot point in the planning process, where your attention shifts from outward to inward. They capture how you define and present yourself in the world. I have included these identity statements in the **Attune** section because, although they are an internally created element (and could therefore live in **Adapt** instead), I think of them as forming part of the environment to which your plan conforms, rather than being fully malleable in response to your contextual analysis. The identity statements, while not fixed, do not change as frequently as your organizational strategy. Yet they are also a listed as a deliverable because editing them is within your control. They will often be affirmed, tweaked, evolved, or overhauled as a result of the strategic planning process.

This brings us to a key choice you need to make at this stage of the process: Will your existing identity statements be taken as "givens" at the outset, and the new plan moulded to align with them? Or is this the starting point for a renewal of those statements?

If your current statements are known to be stale and/or a poor reflection of who your organization is becoming, you may choose to start from scratch. If so, crafting new ones becomes your next task.

If, however, you think your existing identity statements are strong and accurate, or even "good enough for now," then I would suggest leaving them as is and revisiting them at a later stage. Once you have a draft plan in place, you can edit the identity statements to reflect insights gleaned during the planning process. These are usually minor refinements that might make the wording more accurate or shift the emphasis slightly — rarely more major than that, although it can happen. Or, you may do that same check of the statements against the plan and affirm that the statements continue to resonate as they are.

I do not recommend setting out to "tweak" your identity statements at the beginning of your planning process — either overhaul them, or leave them alone for now. People find it very difficult to make small improvements to foundational elements without something concrete against which to assess the proposed changes. Plus, your team is just getting started on this planning journey, and a small revision to identity is a difficult starting point. The group can easily get mired in doing more than a tweak very quickly. You want your process to start with progress (as James Clear says, "success is the best motivator"[88]), and you risk doing the opposite. Overhaul them or leave them alone.

KEY QUESTION

What impact do we exist to have in the world?

HOW TO

Know your "why".

In this section, I will walk you through two ways to develop identity statements as if from scratch. If you are choosing the "tweak or affirm" option, hop down to the end of this section where I will describe a process for doing so.

My first tip for creating new identity statements is not to get stuck in vocabulary. Keep the language very straightforward and don't try to label the statements too soon. In real life, what I mean is this: When someone says, with a scrunchy face, "Is this a mission or a vision?" your answer at this stage can be, "Yes!" Don't worry about accurate labels yet.

Here's the first way to develop an identity statement that combines mission, vision, and values. You'll see that it is a mission statement with a "why" built in. I prefer this to writing a separate vision statement, but that is up to you. The "how" phrases point to organizational values, expressed in behaviours. That's how I prefer to write values, but again, that's up to you.

I'd suggest planning two sessions for this element, of about 90 to 120 minutes each, involving the Steering Committee and perhaps your full Board of Directors.

To develop an identity statement from scratch...

Step one: Introduce the session as being about defining your organization's "big why." You may want to start by showing the group some examples of other organizations' identity statements as inspiration, and asking them what they do or don't like about them. I have included some examples on the following page.

Ask people to answer the following questions:

1. What does our organization exist to provide?

2. For whom? (This could be in terms of audience and/or geography)

3. In order to make what impact or difference?

4. What's important to us about how we provide that service?

If you are doing this exercise in person, I would suggest putting people's answers to each question up on a wall or flipchart in real time. (If you have asked these questions digitally and/or asynchronously, you can post the responses on a wall after the fact for a smaller group to analyze the input — the process is roughly the same).

Step two: Facilitate a conversation that includes the following three questions:

1. How aligned are we in our responses?

2. What repeated themes or words do you notice?

3. Are you noticing any contradictions?

Highlights or repeated themes can be captured visually on a flip chart for the whole group to see. You might also want to ask the group if there is any particular language they do *not* want to see in the final statements.

Selected examples of identity statements

NIKE
- Mission: Bring inspiration and innovation to every athlete* in the world.
  *If you have a body, you are an athlete.
- Our purpose is to unite the world through sport to create a healthy planet, active communities and an equal playing field for all.

IKEA
- Vision: to create a better everyday life for the many people.

Facebook
- Mission: To give people the power to build community and bring the world closer together.

Starbucks
- Mission: To inspire and nurture the human spirit — one person, one cup and one neighborhood at a time.

Tesla
- Mission: To accelerate the world's transition to sustainable energy.

Food Banks Canada
- Vision: A Canada where no one goes hungry.
- Mission: We provide national leadership to relieve hunger today and prevent hunger tomorrow in collaboration with the food bank network in Canada.

United Way of Canada
- Mission: To improve lives and build community by engaging individuals and mobilizing collective action.

Toronto Transit Commission
- Mission: To provide a reliable, efficient and integrated bus, streetcar and subway network that draws its high standards of customer care from our rich traditions of safety, service and courtesy.

City of Vancouver
- Mission: Create a great city of communities that cares about our people, our environment, and our opportunities to live, work, and prosper.

Step three: Invite each person to review the lists generated in the previous step and consider the conversation you've just had. Now ask them to write two sentences that capture the best of what they've heard, in roughly the following format:

Organization _XXX_
exists to _WHAT_
for _WHO / WHERE_,
so that _WHY_.
You can count on us
to do that in ways that _HOW_,
HOW and _HOW_.

You will notice that this format puts your mission, key audiences, purpose and core values into a single statement. Gather these up and check how similar they are across your team.

Step four: Do not finalize written documents in groups larger than about four people! Wordsmithing in a group is excruciating. Instead, give the pile of suggested statements to a small writing team for later. But before you send them on their way, ask the full group one more question:

Let's give the writing team some advice and guidance. What do you want to be true about the draft statement(s) they bring back to us?

Make a list of the characteristics and criteria the group suggests and ask the writers to take those into consideration when they come back to the group with suggestions.

Step five: (This step will take place some time later, after the writers have had a chance to do their work, but not too long after — perhaps a week.) Have the writing group present suggestions to the team. Invite the team first to rate the drafts based on the criteria they have given the writers. For instance, if they asked that the statements be clear and inspiring and sound like "us," they could give each statement a score out of 10 for clarity, for inspiration, and for familiarity of tone. You can do this visually, so that everyone can see the scores at the same time, or individually if confidentiality is important.

Do a quick tally of the scores. You may find that one version has already emerged as the clear "winner" or "leader." If so, you can work further with only that one. If not, you can proceed with the two or three most popular options.

Ask the group:

1. What do you love about this version?
2. Specifically, what would you change about it if it were up to you to draft the final version? (Think format, content, and tone.)

Again, capture this input visually for all to see.

Here's where the rest of the process becomes difficult to describe in advance. You may be basically finished because the feedback is enthu-siastic and clearly aligned across the whole group. Or you may wish to send the writing group back to try again, armed with the feedback they've received. Or something in between. Don't belabour it at this stage — it's time to get it done, at least in draft. You can come back to it later if there are still some rough edges to smooth out.

To invite feedback on existing statements...

Here is a variation on the above, useful if you have a bit less time available and/or perhaps a clearer sense already of how you'd like your current statements to change. You can use it to gather feedback on your ideas rather than inviting the group to create new statements from scratch.

Step one: Identify a handful of specific changes you would like to propose for your current identity statements, or questions you'd like to ask the group about them. For instance, there might be one value in your list of corporate values that seems out of place, a shift in emphasis may be needed in your mission statement, or perhaps you've realized that your vision statement is never used and may not be needed.

Step two: Choose how you would like to gather input — digitally, in person, or both. You can then craft questions to suit your chosen medium. These questions should be designed to gather feedback on the changes you're most interested in. Here are some examples for inspiration:

- Our Mission Statement currently says X. It might sound more accurate/up to date if it said Y instead. On a scale of 1 to 10, how much do you like this proposed change? Explain your answer.

- The term Y in our list of values is not one that we seem to use or talk much about. Although Y is of course a worthwhile concept, it may not be central to our identity anymore. I'm wondering about replacing it with Z because [reason]. What do you think? (Yes/No — Please explain.)

- We've used the same Mission, Vision, and Values list for 17 years and although they contain important ideas, the language admittedly seems a bit stale. I have rewritten the core elements of those statements into this refreshed "elevator pitch" to introduce ourselves. Can you please read this aloud and tell me specifically what you like and don't like about it?

- It's easy for people to get confused about Mission and Vision statements, so I'm recommending we combine ours into a single statement as follows: [statement]. I like it because it sounds both concrete and inspiring, and I think people would remember it. What do you think?

When gathering input, tell people what you plan to do with it. Be clear about the decision-making process that will ensue — who will make the final decision and based on what factors.

Step three: Once you've collated the responses and made a decision in alignment with what you told people to expect, circle back to them with the final version (or at least the next draft) and your rationale for proposing it. Doing what you said you would do builds trust. Close the loop.

To evaluate your identity statements against your new plan...

If you are at the stage of wanting to confirm or tweak your identity statements against a newly developed plan, you could use a variation of the exercise described above, or try this one.

Step one: Post or present the highlights of the new strategic plan, and/or key discussion themes that have emerged during its development, alongside your current identity statements.

Step two: Decide how open-ended you would like the input to be. One possibility is to ask a couple of broad questions, such as "How well aligned is the new strategy with our identity statements?" and "If you were to make one specific change to put these two documents into better alignment, what would that change be?" (Notice that people could choose to change the identity statement or the strategy — the question does not specify.) You'll learn a lot.

Alternatively, you can be more targeted in your questions, by asking something like: "During the planning process, we realized that at its core, our organization is about X and what really lights us up is Y. How well do these identity statements reflect that?" Then you can ask for scores (easily to tabulate but offer little understanding), narrative answers (which are the opposite: difficult to process but deep on nuance), or both to help you finalize the documents.

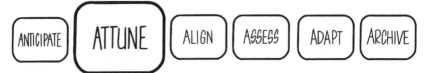

- Contextual analysis
- Identity statements
- Theory of Change

THEORY OF CHANGE

DELIVERABLE

A brief, visually attractive summary of the impact your organization intends to have and the inputs, activities, and outcomes you believe it will take to get there.

DECISION

What you believe about how change happens.

A "Theory of Change" (ToC) is a narrative and visual description of how and why a desired change is expected to occur in a particular context. It explains the linkages between activities and outcomes, usually within a complex and dynamic system. The term comes out of the evaluation field and is used extensively in work on collective impact. It was popularized by Carol Weiss[89] in the mid-1990s and has gained considerable traction since then.

A ToC is not always included in organizational strategic planning processes, but I am increasingly finding it a useful tool for my clients, so I include a brief description of it here in case it appeals to you, too. You may wish to explore some of the literature and examples around Theories of Change to decide whether you want one for your organization at this time.[90] Even more than the outcome, I find that the process of crafting a ToC is a rich learning experience. It's full of struggle, "aha!" moments, and surprises. Tread carefully, because it's not a step to be taken lightly, but if you are committed to its value, I am confident your ToC development process will not disappoint.

I think of a ToC as a place where an illustrated story meets a logic model, all within a context of many complex moving parts. It's called a theory because it is just that — a series of hypotheses that describe how your organization believes change happens. It allows you to summarize the problem you are trying to address, the specific impact your organization will have on that problem, and the assumptions you are making about the relationships between activities and outcomes along the way. It is usually presented both visually and narratively, not simply as a matrix or linear flow chart. It allows you to make your assumptions visible and to identify the specific points at which your organization intends to intervene to make change happen.

You need to be clear on the difference between your theory of change and your strategy. Your ToC is bigger than your strategic plan. It covers a longer time span and exceeds the scope of a single planning cycle. The strategy is a subset of the ToC, both chronologically, in that it might represent a one, three-, or five-year time frame within that longer theory, and in terms of scope, since the organization itself could represent just one actor among many who would implement the desired social change.

Another distinction is a Theory of Change does not necessarily reflect the same level of choice-making as a strategy. It provides an organizational context for your plan that allows you to say, "Here's the big picture of what we are trying to do. Therefore, for the next few years, our focus needs to be on these pieces of the larger puzzle of our emerging strategic plan." Just as a strategic plan (time-bound priorities) nests inside an organization's mission statement (why it exists), so too does it nest inside its ToC (how it believes activities lead to impacts). These various statements should be very much aligned, but they should not be used interchangeably.

Sounds simple, right?

It can be, but developing a ToC can also surface contradictions that are difficult to manage. You may find, for example, that the members of your leadership team hold very different views about the organization's core contribution or even about the problem it is trying to solve. Or, you may notice that your team's assumptions about how change happens are based on an outdated worldview or faulty analysis of the evidence, which has led to programming decisions that are off the mark. Not easy conversations to have, but wouldn't you rather know?

PRO TIP

Lean into the contradictions and pressure points that will arise in your strategy-making conversations. Don't be afraid. They are likely to reveal tensions and imbalances that need to be addressed and that will ultimately make your strategy stronger. As Bill Staples writes, "Understanding contradiction is the key to developing effective strategy."[91]

Let me give you a couple of examples. These are composites of various real ToC conversations I have had with clients in recent months.

There was once an organization founded on scientific research in a particular field. They did it in various ways at multiple levels and were very skilled at it. Yet when they worked through a ToC, they realized that although their activity was very clear (i.e. research), the link between that activity and their desired impact was quite weak. In fact, they were not in agreement about that impact at all. Some considered "a larger body of research" to be their impact, while others wanted "information sharing," or "policy change," or "conservation action." Moreover, they realized that their efforts were based on an implicit assumption that improved evidence would lead to improved evidence-based decision-making — an assumption that was becoming increasingly difficult to stand by, given the current political climate in which they worked. They therefore realized that "knowledge mobilization" needed to become a more prominent organizational pillar, to link their research more deliberately with the changes they wanted to see. Investment in building their knowledge mobilization capacity then became a strategic priority.

I have worked with several anti-poverty groups whose ToC process brought to light that their programming model was based on a theory of trickle-down economics that has long been out of favour. They realized they needed to reorient their approach to governance and service provision to align more closely with what they already knew and promoted about what it actually takes to shift economic inequalities. They were too close to the details to see what had evolved over time — until they had it visually presented back to them through some skilled facilitation.

This is where the strategic planning process becomes iterative, despite often being described in a linear fashion. As described in *Transformational Strategy,* the process tends to deepen like a spiral.[92] Your ToC will shed light on the strategic directions, goals, and key activities you want to pursue over the next planning cycle while also being shaped by what you already do. It sits underneath your identity statements, since it determines how you work that identity out in practice to make a difference in the world, but at times it may seem even bigger than your organization or cause you to adjust how you describe your work to others. Hold the sequence loosely as you work back and forth between the elements.

KEY QUESTION

How do we understand the link between our actions and the changes we most want to influence?

HOW TO

Working hypotheses.

Theories of Change provide a valuable opportunity to invite community partners to join you at the planning table, to check your assumptions, or even to plan at a system-wide scale. Internally, it is helpful to have big-picture thinkers in the room who are skilled at making connections between seemingly disparate elements.

Developing a well-thought-out ToC usually takes a few facilitated workshop sessions, and there are several ways to get there. This is one stage in the planning process where I would usually recommend hiring outside facilitation assistance, for three reasons:

1. You may be too close to the subject matter to be able to guide the group to new insights.

2. You may not want to lose one of your key people to the facilitation task, electing instead to let all of your leaders participate without having to think about navigating the process.

3. You simply may not have anyone in-house with the facilitation skills required to ensure this element gets generated productively. It's a task where groups are prone to getting stuck in what Sam Kaner calls "the groan zone,"[93] and you need someone who can clear a sightline out of it.

With these caveats in mind, four elements really help in the facilitation of a ToC:

1. Start with a template.

2. Make it visual.

3. Be clear about scale.

4. Check for alignment.

1. Start with a template

There are lots of useful ways to structure a ToC, so it helps if you choose just one of them and invite your team to fill in the template. This gives the group a clear destination and a shared understanding of the task in front of them. If, in the process of filling in that template, you discover you need different categories or other ways of depicting your story, you can simply modify the template. You aren't obligated to stick to it, but using one as a shared and explicit jumping-off point is easier than starting from a blank page. There are software tools available to help you build your theory of change, although they may not explicitly help you facilitate the group process for doing so.[94]

2. Make it visual

The final product of a ToC should be visually compelling and sharp, but the process of developing it can also be highly visual. It is generally true in facilitation that making things visible helps a group to stay on track because a shared depiction of a concept on a screen or wall allows mental models to be made explicit and therefore open for examination. Developing a ToC is no exception. Plus, when things inevitably get a bit complicated, working from a single, visible version as you make your refinements helps you stay on track more easily than working only verbally or individually on paper.

3. Be clear about scale

Confirm the scope of what you are collaboratively generating. Is this an organizational ToC or a program-level one? To what extent is your organization responsible for achieving the whole of the ToC versus just one part of it? Over what period of time?

4. Check for alignment

As you refine your emerging ToC, an important question to ask is: "If all of these things happen, and only these things happen, will they lead to the outcome we say they will?" Check your assumptions at each stage and ensure that the logic and comprehensiveness of your ToC remain intact throughout various revisions and iterations.

"The soul...never thinks without a picture."
— Aristotle —

- Positioning
- Strategic pillars
- Goals
- Objectives
- Performance standards
- Key activities

If you drive a car, you've probably had your mechanic recommend an "alignment" as preventative maintenance. Perhaps, like me, you really didn't have a clear understanding of why it was necessary, other than ensuring that all four tires are pointing in the same direction.

An alignment gives you a smoother ride by ensuring that the tires are wearing evenly. This allows you to use less energy to go farther and lowers your risk of a blowout. Without it, you'd probably notice pull or drift in a particular direction rather than travelling in a straight line.

In strategic planning, alignment has similar benefits. You want to make sure that your resources are being used evenly, that the ride is smooth, that you can expend less energy to go further, and that you're avoiding a blowout, all while making sure that you're not pulling or drifting in a direction you don't intend to go.

Once you are attuned to your environment, it's time for your organization to decide how it will align to what it's hearing. Strategic choice making is particularly critical in this phase as you determine which elements of the environment are going to shape your activities. If the **Attune** phase is about listening, the **Align** phase is about choosing.

Having tuned into the broad context that is bigger than your strategy, it is now time to align your strategic decisions with the elements of that context that you deem most relevant. You are moving from description to decision; from information to interpretation.

Strategic Plan Outline: Positioning Statements

POSITIONING

DELIVERABLE

A series of positioning statements along the lines of: "Because of X, we must position ourselves as Y in order to Z."

DECISION

Relevance.

This stage marks the moment where you reorient your planning gaze more internally and begin straddling the outer and inner worlds, with positioning acting as the pivot point.

Positioning is about being known for something and/or having something clearly in your sights. In private sector marketing, positioning is the place your brand occupies relative to others in the minds of consumers. The same can be true in a non-profit context, particularly if you are competing with other worthy causes for philanthropic attention.

But positioning can also be seen as the series of decisions that emerge from your interpretation of contextual data. It's the big "and therefore…" that links your environment to your plan at this time. It's where you draw the sightline between what's happening in the world, what's happening in your organization, and your organization's chosen activities over the next planning cycle.

It's a planning step that often gets missed. But it is a critical step, in part because the same set of data can be interpreted in various ways.

"The task of leadership is to create an alignment of strengths in ways that make a system's weaknesses irrelevant."

— Peter Drucker —

For instance, if you note that rapid technological changes are a key feature of your context, members of your team could legitimately draw different conclusions about the implications of that trend for your organization. Does it mean you should become better at delivering your services digitally? Might you all permanently work from home? Will you market more aggressively to get your market's attention in a noisy online space? Could you use big data to accelerate your delivery time?

Positioning reminds us that purpose by itself is not strategy (see *The Purpose Revolution*[95]). When you have determined your organization's mission and gained a broad understanding of what is needed for change to occur, positioning — how you want to position yourself within your context — is the next big strategic choice.

The narrative goes something like this:

> "Given what is true about our current context at multiple levels;
> And in light of what we are hearing from our key stakeholders;
> And taking into consideration our identity and best contribution(s) as an organization;
> And given our understanding of what it will take for the change we want to see in the world to happen;
> We therefore must increasingly position ourselves as..."

For instance, if your environmental scan has identified changes in government funding and philanthropic patterns as trends relevant to your organization, your positioning conversation creates space to discuss the "so what?" of those trends for you. Might you seek to generate your own revenue or diversify your revenue sources as a result? Or reduce your dependence on public funds? Or...? Similarly, if you are aware that two competitor organizations are struggling, your positioning conversation might help you decide whether you will ensure your agency is seen as "best of breed" in your competitive class, or whether your stance will be to partner with them to bolster your combined effectiveness across your community. Any of these strategic choices are legitimate, but they need to emerge from deliberate dialogue and choice making, all with a view of strengthening your organization's relevance.

KEY QUESTION

***Given what's going on, who we are, and
what we do, what must we pay attention to
and become known for in this planning cycle?***

———

HOW TO

And therefore...

Helping a group reach positioning decisions involves summarizing and
reviewing all you've learned, heard, and created so far and inviting
people to start thinking about the "so what?" of it all.

As with the Identity Statement, you can use a variation of Mad Libs
to structure the group's thinking. People work in pairs or threes to
fill in the following sentence, which is provided to them on cards. I
usually invite them to complete at least one and no more than four
cards per team, depending on the size of the group.

> "Given X, our organization must [increasingly] position itself
> as Y over the next planning cycle in order to Z."[96]

X is usually a description of a trend or evolving situation. Y is usually an adjective or a noun that describes what the organization is
becoming great at and/or known for, and Z provides an additional
rationale for that choice, if needed.

You then gather, post, and analyze the responses with the group. As in
other steps, pay attention to repetition and/or contradictions within

the feedback. Usually obvious clusters emerge that will evolve into shared positioning statements. Conversation then needs to focus on any outliers. Ideally, you will end up with between one and five statements that indicate how your team is choosing to interpret and apply the contextual information that has been collected. Resist the urge to wordsmith these too carefully at this stage. Be precise in intent, but leave the writing and editing for a smaller writing team to do later.

Your positioning statements may no longer be needed by the time the full plan is complete. They will have served their purpose in helping you to clarify your goals, objectives, and so on. Yet for some organizations, this exercise actually proves to be an inflection point in the planning process. Something clicks for the group such that not only is the rest of the process easier from that point, but the positioning statements emerge as core to the eventual plan.

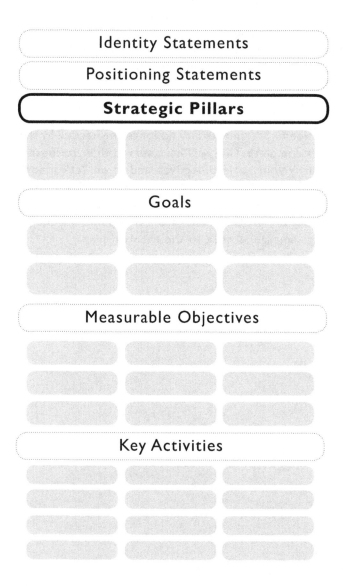

Strategic Plan Outline: Strategic Pillars

ANTICIPATE ATTUNE **ALIGN** ASSESS ADAPT ARCHIVE

- Positioning
- Strategic pillars
- Goals
- Objectives
- Performance standards
- Key activities

STRATEGIC PILLARS

DELIVERABLE

**Categories of work and the direction
or intention you hold for each.**

This is where you start writing the meat of your strategy. You begin identifying the categories of work that need attention. These pillars may be provisional — unlikely to appear in this form in your final plan — or, at the other end of the spectrum, they could end up as the final categories by which your plan is organized.

DECISION

Scaffolding for the strategy.

Before we dive into the specifics of this step, let's talk again about language. Don't get stuck on vocabulary. We are about to address "strategic pillars." These could equally be called intents, strategic directions, priorities, goals.... The specific label or title does not matter. Pick something that seems clear to you for now and stick with it throughout the process. The important part is to avoid confusion and a lack of progress. Shared vocabulary in the room and throughout the life of your plan can be a useful unifying force, but get too hung up on it and it risks being the opposite.

In order to position your organization in the ways you've now described, you will inevitably face a handful of key shifts or challenges that require your attention over the next planning cycle. You probably knew what they were from the outset, and they may have been gnawing at you for a while. Where must you focus your gaze? What parts of the organization most need your attention over the next few years?

Before diving further into this question, another requires a response first: will your new strategic plan cover everything your organization does (including your core business), or just your areas of strategic focus for this planning period? Or do those two categories actually overlap almost completely for you?

You may have put this question to rest already, as we talked about it as the "ambition" of the plan from the outset. Now is the time to make sure you're sure.

I have worked with organizations that have successfully developed and implemented strategic plans on both sides. There is no single right way to proceed, but it is likely that you could identify strategic priorities within each of your key business areas such that the circles of the Venn diagram overlap considerably. A comprehensive plan feels more integrated and more reflective of real life. Generally, your plan should reflect the full scope of your organization without describing every detail of what you do. Rather, your plan should be sharply targeted within each of your core business areas. Strategic planning is about making choices, not laundry lists. As shown in the figure above, if there are elements of your current business not found in your strategy, it should be because you have chosen to leave them behind.

KEY QUESTION
———

What are the "big buckets" of work that will structure our strategy?

———

HOW TO
———
Big buckets.

For this step and the following ones within the **Align** category, I usually recommend working with the Steering Committee or some other group of perhaps five to twelve people comprising of Directors and staff. It is useful to have the same group of people present throughout this cluster of steps to ensure consistency.

You can once again either start with a blank slate or customize a template. What you are aiming for are the large categories or pillars of your plan — I call them "big buckets" — with a notional statement of what you would like to see happen within each.

Resist the urge to get too specific too soon. Common categories include, for example, programming or product development, revenue model/fundraising, corporate culture, organizational systems, recruitment and retention of talent, governance, growth trajectory, value proposition to customers/investors/members/clients, and facilities/capital.

Rather than thinking functionally, you could also choose to approach this task thematically, considering categories such as innovation, sustainability, alignment with values, and so on.

To get there, consider asking the group, "To achieve our desired positioning, what topics or areas definitely require our attention?"

You can invite participants to work alone or in small groups to write individual ideas on post-it notes. You will likely find that the ideas vary widely in terms of altitude. That is fine at this point, as you will not be treating each one individually quite yet — they are simply intended to populate emerging categories. The post-its can then be clustered into themes, and the titles of the clusters become the starting point for your strategic pillars.

Now consider, in broad terms, what you are going after within each. More or less of something? A faster or slower cadence? Focus or breadth? Add some directionality to your intention.

Examples of strategic directions might include, "Greater resource diversification," "Higher board engagement," "Stronger evident commitment to diversity, equity and inclusion," or "Assurance of program quality." These will become the pillars of your plan.

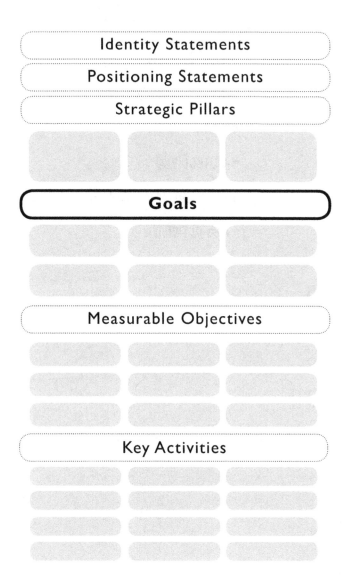

Strategic Plan Outline: Goals

- Positioning
- Strategic pillars
- Goals
- Objectives
- Performance standards
- Key activities

GOALS

DELIVERABLE

——

Goals with parallel construction, all at a similar strategic altitude.

DECISION

——

What to pursue.

If you think of the strategic planning process as gradually travelling from the wide end of a funnel to the narrow end, with ever-increasing specificity, then goal setting is the bridge between the general and the specific. It is where you give your positioning statements "legs" by describing what you intend to accomplish.

Before we get into the specifics of how to develop goals within your plan, I would like to zoom out and talk about goal setting as an enterprise. Much has been written about the merits or pitfalls of goals, perhaps most notably by Locke and Latham in their *Theory of Goal Setting*[97] and then in a rebuttal called *Goals Gone Wild* by Ordóñez et al[98], in which the authors identify the serious, systematic, and predictable harmful side effects of goal setting in organizations. Oliver Burkeman continues this conversation in his fine book *The Antidote*,[99] drawing on work by people such as Christopher Kayes,[100] Stephen Shapiro,[101] and Brian Tracy.[102] He reminds us that goals are useful, but should not be considered in isolation because in achieving one goal, you are invariably changing the system in which those goals are situated. He talks about the danger of pursuing one goal successfully but destroying other important things in the process. (We've all heard of the marathon runner who successfully runs the race, but destroys his marriage in the meantime). Goals can become obsessions when they become synonymous with our identity, to the point that we pursue them not just in the face of contrary evidence, but even perhaps because of that evidence. Burkeman highlights the compelling tale of climbers dying on Mount Everest to make his point.

Like many polite Canadians, I find myself on the fence in this conversation. I believe goal setting is very important as a motivator (although Burkeman would say that sometimes visualizing the achievement of our goals actually makes us less motivated to do the work required to achieve them!).

Goal Setting

I think of people achieving goals in three different ways. Some people set a huge, audacious goal because they figure that if they if don't reach it, they will still have made very impressive progress. This reminds me of my friend Col Fink, who set himself the gutsy goal of making the world championship ultimate frisbee team, because he figured that even if he only made the Australian national team, that would still be amazing. He did end up making that world team, against significant odds, and he knows that if he hadn't set himself that goal, he never would have made it.

A mid-range goal setter often sets goals they know they'll be able to achieve — just. That way they don't over or undershoot. This might be the person who crawls their way to the finish line right at the deadline, but gets there.

Other people approach goals in a more modest way, saying, "I know I have until December to reach my annual goals, but I'll set them such that I can confidently reach them by April, making any achievement throughout the rest of the year just 'gravy.' I'll feel like an overachiever!"

At one time I would have suggested that each of your goals should sit in the same range, rather than having some be at the moonshot level and others be quite basic. But now my advice is to have an explicit conversation about the reach of each one of your goals, and to make the choice deliberate. If, in doing so, you identify one moonshot goal that requires the rest of your strategy to be modest, so be it.

I am a fan because I think goals give us a clear direction in which to travel. I'm an even bigger fan because goals provide a means by which to set that direction collaboratively. Our mental models of what we're trying to achieve and where we are trying to end up need to be made explicit around the planning table so that they can be pressure tested, examined, and refined, and ultimately brought into a single point of focus so that our destination can ultimately become a filter through which we make decisions. To the extent that strategy allows us to say no to things, goals act as an initial screening tool.

If we simply look one step ahead rather than several steps ahead, we may be faithfully taking one step in front of the other, ahead and ahead, toward a destination we didn't want to go to at all. We know from physics and space travel that being off by just a couple of degrees at the beginning of a long journey can lead us to literally land on the wrong planet. So it's important to be very clear on your sightline from the outset. But by the same token, even if your bearings are perfect, you can't simply put the aircraft on autopilot and hope for the best. You need to be prepared to respond to all sorts of obstacles and complications along the way that might have knocked you off your initial bearing. That's why strategic planning is both an art and a science: we need to be clear about what we're trying to accomplish, but we also need to be flexible and responsive in how we're going to get there. Goals need to have both a fixed and malleable quality. That's where the artistry of strategic planning comes in.

I also believe that goals should be adjusted in response to context. If we have no way of knowing that the context is changing in relevant ways that might cause us to adjust our sightline, then our goals can cease to be relevant without us even realizing. In such cases, I'm not convinced that the goals themselves are the problem, though our cognitive biases and inclinations both to pursue them too doggedly or not doggedly enough do of course need to be taken into account. Organizations that have reliable, innovative ways of checking in on what their audiences most need and adjusting their business model in response are best placed to decide when their goals, or perhaps just the means to achieving them, need to be revamped. This is what I referred to on page 79 as "reconnaissance capacity."

At this point in the process, or maybe at later stages topic by topic, you and your team will need to decide which knots you most need to

untangle. I am a knitter, so I've had my share of experience unscram-
bling impossibly tangled balls of wool. You don't do it all at once. You
don't take the whole thing and start grabbing at it from the middle
and yanking. You tease it apart gently, keeping your fingers light, and
you find individual knots. By untangling those one at a time, as you
wind the ball up gradually, you eventually find that you can wind the
whole thing.

Similarly, in strategic planning, goals are often shaped by identifying
the key knots to untangle within each pillar. Playing to Win[103] presents
examples of this process in the private sector context, specifically
for the consumer goods company Procter and Gamble. The authors
highlight the decision-making process related to a lagging skincare
line. P&G had to decide if they should shut down that product line,
acquire a new one, move one of their other products into that line,
or choose one of five or six other possibilities. That's what I mean
by "knots." It's not enough to say, "We need to talk about governance
(or programming, or resource development)." At some point you
need to identify what it is inside those categories that most needs
to be wrestled with. You need to bravely get in the ring before you
can set your goals. Strategy is "a cohesive response to an important
challenge — [and] without knowing the challenge, you can't assess
the quality of the strategy."[104]

This is one area where the planning process can take longer than
you might think, because you might have some seriously tangled
yarn! I've seen groups wisely decide that certain knots are going
to be untangled later rather than during the planning process itself,
and they add the untangling of that particular knot to their plan as
an objective or activity. Other groups say, "We've got two or three
huge knots to address right now. For the many other small ones,
let's just wind them into the ball and deal with them when we get
to them in our actual knitting." Fair enough. Proportionality comes
into play here, but you don't want to skip this step, because you
may miss out on having the brave conversations you most need to
have by jumping too quickly to making decisions. Instead, have the
courage to walk together through the foggy territory of deciding
which decisions need to be made in order to plan, and which ones
can become part of the plan.

Then, once you've identified the knots that do need to be untangled sooner rather than later, ask what the Heath brothers call "the miracle question: Imagine the problem were miraculously solved — what would be different?"[105] Your response will help you get at your goals. To look at it another way: What is the breakthrough we need?

Don't nail down your goals too soon. Consider many possibilities. It's like planning a trip — there are lots of great vacation destinations, and at first you need to browse some sites and gather some recommendations. The Heath brothers warn against narrow framing of decisions: "What's in the spotlight will rarely be everything we need to make a good decision, but we won't always remember to shift the light. Sometimes in fact we'll forget there's a spotlight at all."[106] Mintzberg issues a similar warning:[107] Identify many possibilities, and then ask, as Lafley and Martin do in *Playing to Win* "What would have to be true for this idea or possibility to be amazing?"[108] Answers to this question, particularly from your resident sceptics, allow you to begin shortening your odds and your list.

I once worked with an interior designer called Rosemary it was known that when you hired Rosemary you should be patient. Her first idea was amazing and her second idea even better, but if you could stay noncommittal and unattached to those early ideas, often her third or fourth idea was the one that hit it out of the park. Too often when we are seeking to generate a focused document under time pressure, we don't allow enough time at appropriate stages for ideation. We want to get to a solution too soon. Goal setting does not sound like a creative brainstorming exercise and yet there are many roads that lead toward your destination. This is the stage to wander down several of them at least a little way, and see what you can see.[109]

James Clear expresses this ironic, emergent quality of goal setting well:

> "The idea here is to commit to your goal with the utmost conviction. Develop a clear, single-minded focus for where you're headed. Then, however, you do something strange. You release the desire to achieve a particular outcome and focus instead on the slow march forward.

Pour all of your energy into the journey, be present in the moment, be committed to the path you're walking. Know that you're moving unwaveringly in one clear direction and that this direction is right for you, but never get wrapped up in a particular result or achieving a certain goal by a specific time.

In other words, your goal becomes your compass, not your buried treasure. The goal is your direction, not your destination. The goal is a mission that you're on, a path that you follow. Whatever comes from that path — whatever treasure you happen to find along the journey — well, that's just fine. It is the commitment to walking the path that matters."[110]

KEY QUESTION

What do you want to be different at the end of this planning cycle compared to what is true now? (Or more succinctly: What are we doing after?)

HOW TO

Attention to achieve intention.

One way to craft goals is to divide your planning team into smaller groups (unless you have five or fewer people participating) and invite them to consider the question, "What are we going after?" within each of the strategic pillars. They will likely break each pillar into smaller topics as per the example below, each of which can be turned into a goal.

Strategic pillar: Financial resources

Possible topics: Amount, diversification, blend of funding types

Groups find it helpful to be given a loose formula or mini-script to follow; it focuses their efforts and ensures the outputs are parallel in construction, making them easier to compare and contrast. Michael Wilkinson suggests using a "verb plus object plus purpose" model for goals which I have found useful so long as the goals remain results-oriented.[111] In practice, it means inviting people to consider at a high level what they will do to achieve a desired result. To follow on with our example:

Topic	Goals
More money	Increase and redeploy combined revenue from all sources in order to have sufficient resources to fulfil our strategic priorities.
More funders	Reduce vulnerability by lowering our dependence on a single funder.
More funding types	Diversify our funding portfolio to expand our reach. Build internal capacity in philanthropic giving in order to attract resources from corporate foundations. Optimize return on internal fundraising investment.

There are a couple of things to note about these examples.

First, the "topics" may not appear in the final plan in this form. They are simply placeholders at this point, tools to structure the conversation of your group(s) to make sure that each of the elements of the pillars features in the discussion. As the facilitator, you can break the task down for the group by saying, "Take your big strategic pillar, break it into topical chunks, then use the goal template to identify one to three goals within each topic."

The other thing to notice is that these goals reflect broad intended results. While you may choose to attach measurability to them at this point, I have elected to insert metrics at the level of objectives, which come later. We are going to discuss performance metrics in a later step. For now, the most important thing is to determine which topics require strategic-level goals and to express those intentions in draft form.

Once the groups have finished this task, you can bring them back together to present their suggested goals and subject them to a two-layer quality check as a team. If the previous exercise was about thinking "vertically" to make sure the goals align with the pillars, this step encourages "horizontal" thinking to ensure alignment across the organization such that the goals are not working at cross purposes with one another and that, taken together, they represent an appropriate reach.

The first layer of the quality check involves responding to each small group's presentation with the following question, addressed to the whole group, "If we were to accomplish all of the goals within this pillar, would the organization's critical needs within that pillar be fully met?" Then, once all of the goals have been presented, you could ask, "If you were to accomplish all of the goals in the whole plan, and only these goals, over this planning cycle, would you feel successful? Taken together, would this suite of goals constitute an appropriately ambitious, impactful, integrated plan?" These questions help to make sure you are dealing with goals both individually and across the plan. It will become increasingly challenging as you move further into the details of the plan to maintain that higher-level perspective, so now is the time to get it right.

A second layer of quality assurance is to make sure the suggestions are what I call "high-leverage goals," meaning goals that, if achieved, will have disproportionately positive and wide-reaching ripple effects on other things in the organization. Ideally, they would address more than one of your pillars at a time. You're not trying to go for quantity or even full coverage as much as leverage. Three memorable, impactful goals are preferable to twenty goals that scatter your attention. The exercise of presenting all the goals back to the full planning team at once allows the group to remove duplicates or those ideas that belong at a more operational level and prune the list of goals to those that are most needed.

As Steven Covey says, "The main thing is to keep the main thing the main thing"[112]

The above process is one I use frequently, and it will get you there. But my concern is that it tends to produce a plan very similar to the current reality. The process design itself is likely to lead to incremental change. If we ask the same people the same set of clear but relatively safe questions in the same familiar environment, the likelihood of them producing something radically different is low.

What would it look like to run a goal-setting process that is intentionally designed to generate goals that are not similar to the status quo?

Let me propose a second way to produce goals.

I suspect that we would need potentially different people in the room. Asking the people who created or benefit from the status quo, or both, may not yield the results you are looking for.

Truly creative goal setting might require us to imagine a context and a future that sits just outside the edges of our current awareness, and that's a very difficult thing to do.

PRO TIP

Throughout the process, as elements of the strategy evolve, be sure to help the group keep sight of the "golden thread" that links previous steps with future ones. You can use this as an opportunity to do what Bill Staples describes as "checking the resolve of the group" — to assess the extent to which they are clear about and committed to what has been proposed thus far.[113]

Creativity meets strategy

A considerable literature is emerging about the conditions that lead to enhanced creativity, individually and as a team.

Here is a list of ten key words that summarize those factors, which I use to help me remember to build them into my group processes. I've included references in the endnotes in case you want to dig deeper.[114]

Positivity Asking appreciative questions, being optimistic, and feeling hopeful can all help us be more creative.

Presence Being fully present and giving a task our full attention in the spirit of deep work helps bolster creativity.[115]

Parameters Creativity flourishes with edges, constraints, and limitations.

Power Tap into powerful poses, language, and emotions to let your creativity flow.

Prizes Incentives and rewards can help catalyze creativity.

Practice Creativity is the result of quantity not quality when it comes to generating ideas and possibilities.

People Creative people lead creative teams, so surrounding ourselves with inspiring people jumpstarts our creativity.

Protection We need to provide an incubator for our newborn ideas, to let them germinate and grow a little before subjecting them to the wider world.

Problems We are most creative when we are applying our creativity to real-world challenges.

Parental loss Research indicates that, on average, people who have lost one or two parents, particularly early in their lives, are more creative.

And one final tip: creative people walk a lot. It doesn't start with P (promenade?), but it's worth mentioning that walking is apparently good for creativity, as it's something that's available to all of us![116]

One way we can get closer to that imagined future is by asking different questions. Imagine the difference in responses between, "So what should we do?" and "What's the bravest thing we could do?" or "What's the most positively disruptive thing we can do?" or "What's the thing that makes you feel a little sick when you think about it but also gives you sweaty palms in a good way?" The Heath brothers point to a "vanishing options" question such as "You can't choose any of the current options. What could you do?"[117]

Imagine if...
How might we...?
What if we...?
How could we connect *this* with *that*?

Generative language enhances creativity. This is a great time in your planning process to have that kind of conversation.

It's not your typical brainstorming session ("Think of every possible idea... there are no bad ideas... let's blue sky this..."), although you might use that tool at times. It's much more about hosting a strategically creative conversation that intentionally draws your group into a space of innovation, rather than sameness. Not for the sake of change, but to think pointedly about what your organization most needs to do in order to have the impact you want to have in the world.

Let me give you an example.

I once worked with a client that was involved in providing affordable housing. They set themselves a goal of a 100% increase in the housing stock they built over the previous year. They were quite nervous about setting that bigger goal. It sounded quite ambitious.

Until I looked at the actual numbers, that is. They had built seven houses in the previous year, and therefore were looking to build fourteen houses this year. An impressive increase when you benchmark against last year's performance, sure.

But the housing need in their community was larger than that by a factor of 1,000. Maybe even 10,000. Thus, the dent that they were making in the affordable housing market was very small and would continue to be very small, even with a 100% increase.

What would it look like for a group like that to say, "What must we do to make a change in the affordable housing situation in our town?" Deciding strategy based on need might lead them to do very different things than benchmarking against what they've always done.

Cowley and Domb highlight the distinction between seeking to be competitive versus world class.[118] As you think about how to set your goals. I would encourage you to think about the specific questions you ask and what you're benchmarking against. Because if you want to be best in class, you need to surround yourself with people who inspire you to greatness.

Identity Statements

Positioning Statements

Strategic Pillars

Goals

Measurable Objectives

Key Activities

Strategic Plan Outline: Measurable Objectives

- Positioning
- Strategic pillars
- Goals
- Objectives
- Performance standards
- Key activities

OBJECTIVES

DELIVERABLE

Objectives for your goals: the elements, activities, or tasks required to achieve them.

Along the way to finalizing your goals, it is likely that certain elements came up in conversation that weren't exactly goals in and of themselves, but perhaps related to or fell within other goals. You may have even discussed whether they were in fact goals, but decided they did not warrant their own category. Don't lose those! They might belong here, under the heading of **Objectives**.

This is where things get practical. These are steps that take you further into the planning funnel: clusters of activities that, taken together, help you to achieve your goal. They are the components of your goal — the elements required to achieve it. If you were writing an essay, they would be the subpoints supporting your main argument.

One benefit of developing objectives is that they paint a more detailed picture of where you're heading and how you might get there. For those of you who've been troubled by a lack of specificity in the plan thus far, this is the stage where you'll start to feel a bit more comfortable. A way forward is emerging out of the fog!

DECISION

How we are going to get this done.

A key challenge here is to decide not only how to achieve your goals, but how firmly or loosely to hold your objectives once you develop them. Do they represent examples of routes to your desired destination, or the route you're going to take? In the spirit of flexibility, responsiveness, and learning, the former may be preferable. Yet a need for motivation, clear progress, and accountability may lead you toward the latter. The temptation that comes with craving detail is to dive too deep too soon, and then to assume that the specifics are what is truly important to your strategy rather than the results to which they contribute. Straddling the space between results and tactics can be tricky, and that is exactly what objectives require you to do.

Let me offer some examples.

If one of your goals is to be positioned as a recognized thought leader in your field, your objectives could be to be publish a certain number of articles, to be invited to speak at particular conferences, or to participate in selected system-wide advisory boards. For you, those component parts might, taken together, equal thought leadership. For others, those objectives might seem too detailed. They may prefer to articulate a layer in between, with objectives related to becoming known for writing, speaking, and advising. Either can work, but it helps to maintain a comparable level of detail at each layer of the plan. We talked at the beginning about checking for "altitude," and this is a place where you get to do so — but I would suggest that all of your objectives stay on a similar flight path.

If you have established a goal of strengthening your organization's commitment to justice, diversity, equity, and inclusion, your objectives will reflect your priorities amongst the many pathways toward doing so. You might commit to ensuring that people of colour are interviewed for leadership positions. You could work specifically toward greater economic or age diversity on your board. You could commit to conducting a gender audit and implementing the recommended changes. You could invest in organization-wide staff training on these issues. Your specific choices should reflect the current needs of your organization and, taken together, should make substantial progress toward your goal.

If you have a goal of demonstrating stronger leadership in corporate sustainability, your key objective could be to develop a fulsome corporate sustainability strategy and communication plan. Or, you could set more specific objectives that outline the component parts of such a strategy, such as reducing waste, increasing clean energy production, and accelerating your corporation's investment in community betterment. Again, as long as your objectives stay at a similar level of detail, either of these scenarios can work. But know that if you opt for more general objectives now, they will leave you more work to do later. You can decide to use whatever level of detail you want in your strategic document, but either way, execution will have to happen. At some point you will need to land this plane, but you may be comfortable flying at 20,000 feet or 10,000 feet for the moment.

KEY QUESTION

What are the smaller projects that will lead to the achievement of our larger goal?

HOW TO

Building blocks.

When it comes to facilitating the development of objectives, my sticky wall (a piece of nylon fabric sprayed with repositionable adhesive spray, which turns paper into sticky notes and allows you to easily move/cluster notes during a session for participants to see) is my favourite tool. It helps to keep things visual, explicit, and organized. If you don't have one, large post-its will do. You can also replicate this experience digitally using one of many collaborative virtual whiteboard tools.

I post the goals across the top and invite people to identify the components or key activities required to achieve each of them. They write their ideas on individual cards or stickies and post them under the appropriate goal. This can be done individually or in small groups, depending on the size of your group and the breadth of your plan. Providing a couple of examples and a template is helpful in keeping the input comparable across groups. You can also gather any stray activity suggestions from previous discussions and invite participants to post these on the wall, too. This is a great way to create a sense of continuity.

Once all of the ideas are posted visually, you can remove duplicates and cluster them into similar categories. This can be done with the whole group, or you can invite each small group to "tidy up" one goal and present their results back to the full team. This is the point where you will start to see objectives emerging.

As a quick quality check, I usually invite the groups to consider two questions, just as we did for goals.

First, "If we achieved all of these objectives and only these objectives, would we be able to say with confidence that the goal had been adequately achieved?" The second question is "What's missing?" This has two parts. First, are we missing anything that would help us achieve this goal, and second, did we come up with any objectives that we know need to happen but don't currently have a goal "home base"? This serves as an additional quality assurance step for your goals as well, because in the course of conversation, you may discover that there are some important activities you are committed to getting done that don't really fit anywhere yet. This will prompt you to loop back and make sure that your goals are exactly as you want them to be.

Remember to intentionally frame these results for your team so they know how tightly or loosely to hold the objectives at this point!

- Positioning
- Strategic pillars
- Goals
- Objectives
- Performance standards
- Key activities

PERFORMANCE STANDARDS

DELIVERABLE

Measurability within your strategy.

This is where you decide how to assess your progress and what constitutes satisfactory or outstanding achievement. That's what a performance standard does — it indicates how you will measure your achievement and what level of performance you consider to be a win.

Your performance standards reveal your priorities perhaps even more than your goals do. They clarify where you're going to invest your attention and resources based on how much progress you intend to make and how quickly. You have decisions to make about scope and leverage, as you don't want to move too many dials at once. Rather, you want to invest your energy in turning the most impactful ones.[119]

Once finished, you may choose to insert these performance standards into the wording of your objectives, or to leave them as a separate column alongside those objectives.

DECISION

How performance will be measured.

Before you decide on specific measures, there are several other decisions to be made.

First, how critical is measurability to you, and how specific do you want your measures to be? In some contexts, highly quantifiable and verifiable measures are important, whereas in others there is a reluctance even to move in that direction — perhaps because some things are just too difficult to measure with confidence, or because that level of accountability feels threatening or undesirable. It's okay to say that you don't want a plan with very tight measures. You're allowed! This plan is yours, and it's supposed to be helpful to you. What I would suggest, though, is to word your plan such that you have a way of knowing how successful you've been in achieving it or not. That's what measurability is for. If you have no way of developing a shared understanding over time of how close you've gotten to achieving the intentions you've set, then greater measurability is the likely antidote.

I once worked with a government client that was reluctant to put firm numbers against its targets, but knew that its previous plan had not gone far enough toward making its goals measurable. Now, five years later, they really couldn't say with confidence whether they had achieved their earlier plan or not. They wanted this new plan to be one that they could look back on and celebrate as having been achieved — yet they were nervous about committing to specific numbers.

What we did as a compromise was to ask, "Do you want this particular goal area to go up or down, and do you want it to go up or down by a lot or a little bit?" They identified certain elements of the plan that required very ambitious acceleration and concerted action, and other parts of the plan where they were content just to hold steady. They didn't attach percentages or absolute figures to their goals, but they did indicate which particular metrics they wanted to change, in what direction, and by what magnitude.

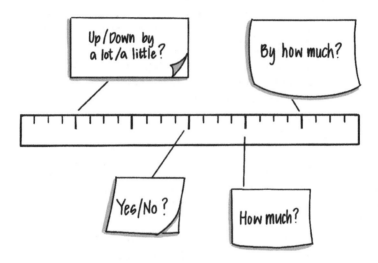

Next, you need to be clear about what level of your plan you are measuring. It is often most tangible to attach measures to your objectives, working within the assumption that if you achieve all of those objectives, you will have achieved your goals. But you may instead choose for the measures to be fewer and attached to your goals, perhaps because the achievement of your objectives is clear without measurability and/or because you are more confident in your goals staying stable over time than your objectives.

This is also the moment to revisit your ambitiousness. Measures make explicit your answers to questions of magnitude and pace. Is your plan super gutsy or pretty modest? Are you preparing to "go big and go fast" or is this planning cycle about changing in small increments? Are you aiming for a similar level of ambitiousness across all of your objectives, or are some of them worthy of greater reach? For some measures, even maintaining the status quo might be considered a win for you at this time. Confirm the level of stretch you're going for before diving into specific numbers.

You may notice that you're circling back to topics that arose earlier in the process. You may discover that there is less consensus around your Steering Team table than you first thought, now that you're getting into the nitty gritty of priority setting. Or perhaps back then it was too early to be able to have those discussions at the level of granularity that you now need. In this regard it's a bit like learning math: in high school, you learn about fractions just like you did in grade five, but the level of complexity gets deeper to match your level of readiness and understanding.

The next key decision is to "know your win" — that is, to work out what success really means to you and your organization. Your actual measures are less important than a shared understanding of what constitutes success. You need to understand what game you're playing.

For me, this is exemplified by a game I sometimes play on my phone when I'm waiting in line. It's a spatial game involving wooden blocks, similar to Tetris. The intent is to fit various shapes into a puzzle as they fall from the sky so that they form horizontal rows. Every time you complete a horizontal row, that row disappears. Ultimately, that's how you win the game. But I can get sucked into playing a different game. I find intricate ways to put the blocks together to make pretty patterns. The problem is, the pretty patterns are often vertical, meaning I usually lose very quickly. Both games are fun; one "wins," one doesn't — at least, not by traditional standards!

Similarly, a business coach from the Thought Leaders Business School program once said to me "Well, Rebecca, if the game you're playing is to demonstrate that you have the capacity to cram as much as possible into your calendar, into every nook and cranny of empty space you have, you would win the game. Unfortunately, that's not the game we're playing here." Sigh.

Measures make explicit your answers to questions of MAGNITUDE and PACE.

A word about vocabulary

Performance standards are often called Key Performance Indicators or KPIs, but I prefer the word "standards" because it implies a benchmark or level of quality that I don't hear in "indicator."

Imagine I tell you it's 15 degrees outside today. What more do you want to know in order to make that piece of information meaningful? I suspect you might ask: Are we talking degrees Fahrenheit or Centigrade? Where in the world are we? Is it July or January? I can assure you that 15 degrees Celsius where I live near Toronto, Canada is a bit chilly for the summer but positively balmy in the midst of winter!

In this example, the temperature is the metric and the thermometer is the indicator we look at to tell us if it is warm or cold outside. But the standard is provided by the context and my own judgement — if it's July where I live, I would probably consider warm to be 25 degrees Celsius or higher, whereas in February, "warm" might be -5.

The same principle holds true in measuring the achievement of your strategic plan. Let's take retention of talent as an example. Your metric might be "churn rate." This is measured by an indicator such as undesirable departures each quarter. You decide which is the most meaningful way to measure churn: is it about the actual number, the percentage of your total staff, or the change in the number over time? The desired performance standard is also set by you. Maybe you are in a highly competitive market, where staying the course at a static level is actually a win. Maybe you are in an industry where staff training is highly specialized and expensive, so you need retention rates to be especially high. Or perhaps you've come through a period of upheaval during which staff have been choosing to leave — in that case, maybe a slowing of the negative churn rate is the best you can hope for.

You likely talked also about aspiration early in the strategy-making process, but it's important to revisit it when you think specifically about performance standards. This is the opportunity for your team to gather and say, "What might we see that would reassure us that we are doing a really good job?" Measurement makes the levels of ambition and aspiration explicit, deliberate, and consistent.

Not surprisingly given its title, the classic strategic planning book *Playing to Win* talks about the importance of being in the game to win. The authors argue you should "choose to win rather than simply play," and that "a too-modest aspiration is far more dangerous than a too-lofty one. Too many companies eventually die a death of modest aspirations."[120] I have to agree. It's hard enough to win if you're trying; if you're not, your chance of winning is very low indeed.

Defining your win might seem simple, but often it's not. In the non-profit and public sectors, it's not always clear what winning actually means or looks like. Some in the community-benefit space might argue that simply playing the game is enough. You don't have to be the best or biggest. If your efforts help some people, that's better than helping no people, and when you have a social purpose mandate, that's a pretty compelling argument. But it makes these conversations about magnitude of change particularly difficult.

For example, if I'm working in food security, I might consider it a win if more people are accessing food, because perhaps that means that my reach is expanding. However, it could also be considered a loss because it implies that more people may be on the verge of going hungry. Without a conversation around the planning table of whether we are aiming for that number to go up or down, people could easily be working at cross purposes with one another about something as basic as what success in your program looks like.

This conversation about winning is made even more difficult by two other factors. In the non-profit space, framing planning in a competitive way could be problematic. Doing so assumes a zero-sum game, where there are clear winners and losers. In a zero-sum game, being a winner necessarily means taking benefits away from the losers, which in your context might be your peers from other agencies or worse, their clients.

Another concern I have with the "playing to win" mentality is that it seems to assume a stable context, a series of problems to which there are known solutions, and perhaps a lower level of complexity than we know to be true.

That said, pursuing excellence and seeking to have a game-changing effect in your space is a compelling aim. The idea of going after mediocrity is not a really strong reason to get up in the morning.

The story goes that a major airline once intentionally set their vision as "satisfactory customer service" for their loyalty points program. Those points were a massive liability for the company, so although they wanted people to accrue them, they wanted to create some intentional friction when it came to redeeming them. They wanted passengers to be excited about having accumulated points, but never to cash them in. They therefore set their sights on mediocre customer service as a disincentive for customers to redeem their points.[121]

While this approach may have made some sense in that industry at that time, most of us don't aspire to be average. We are motivated by success, which implies knowing what that means.

In many settings where I work, I notice that people are working very hard, and are very passionate and earnest. They are mission-motivated. But in the absence of understanding specifically what they're trying to do, or in contexts where they can argue, "Even one life changed is enough," conversations around cost benefit analyses or return on investment have very low resonance. Even the currency of a win is unclear, let alone how much of that currency you'd like to accumulate. Community-benefit spaces, public and non-profit, could benefit from defining more precisely what their currencies are. The very act of having that conversation has enormous learning value and can lead to much greater focus on the organization's most meaningful activities.

Yet another decision around performance standards has to do with bench-marking. To whom or against what will you compare your performance? If you're involved in urban planning and your comparative benchmark is the sleepy town where you grew up, you might do different things, or feel differently about your own performance as a city, than if your benchmark were Singapore or some other world-class, innovative metropolis.

Whom you compare yourself to shapes the aspirations you set for yourself. And it shapes your sightline, because it shapes what you think is possible. It shapes your self-concept, both as a leader and as an organization.

And therefore, it will seep into the measurements you choose. Be careful to measure yourself against inspiring company.

MEASURABILITY DECISIONS

- [ ] How critical is measurability to you?
- [ ] How specific do you need your measures to be?
- [ ] What layer(s) of your plan are you measuring?
- [ ] How ambitious are you seeking to be, overall and within each objective?
- [ ] Are you clear on your win?
- [ ] What or who are you benchmarking against?
- [ ] What has to be true for each performance standard to be a good one?

One final decision is your criteria for choosing performance standards. What needs to be true for them to be judged as "good"? For instance, you may determine that they need to be clearly understood and not overly cumbersome (individually or in aggregate), and that your pace of achievement must be sustainable over time. In order for measurement not to be cumbersome, you may wish to set a numerical limit on how many things you will track. Or, in the early months of your plan, you may want to limit your measurements to things about which you already have reliable baseline data. After all, it's hard to measure progress when you don't know your starting point!

A Sustainable Pace

James Clear talks about putting upper limits on our goals, not just lower limits. So rather than saying, "I'm going to do at least this many push-ups or make at least this many phone calls," we say, "I'm going to do at least x but no more than y." Why would we do that? Because it creates a habit of staying within a sustainable zone that will allow us to grow over the long term. We're making progress without burning out. If you are prone to overdoing it, consider setting upper limits as well as minimum thresholds when you are setting your performance standards.

And (phew!) now we can actually talk numbers.

KEY QUESTION

What level of progress deserves a gold star?

- We are inserting measurability at the level of:

  _____ *(goals/objectives)*

- We are paying attention specifically to:

  _____ *(goal objective)*

- We have confirmed that this cannot be deleted, deferred, or delegated.[122]

  _____ *(yes/no)*

- We have therefore decided to use the following indicator(s) to measure this:

  _____

- We want the following level of specificity:

  _____

  (number, change, direction, magnitude, etc.)

- Do we have a baseline measure?

  _____ *(yes/no)*

- Therefore, over the next year we would like to attain:

  _____ *(results)*

- Over the next three years, we would like to attain:

  _____ *(results)*

- Therefore, our performance standard is:

  _____

  *(to increase X by Y, to achieve an exact number,
  to bring Z down a little, etc.)*

HOW TO

Know your win.

Once the above decisions have been made, you will find the actual setting of performance standards to be quite straightforward. They should include a measurement or direction, a timeframe, and a target. For example, you might choose to increase revenue by 7% over three years or to engage 5,000 new donors by the end of year one of your plan.

The following template is a useful tool for confirming your decisions and setting your performance standards.

You may choose to involve a different combination of people in those initial decisions around measurement than in actually setting the measures. Not everyone is inclined toward this kind of work, so providing some parameters to a small group of people who are wired for measurement, monitoring, and accountability can be a good delegation of labour. Making sure you have the right people working on the right jobs is a key element of getting this done well.

If your group is struggling with coming to a shared understanding of magnitude, pace, and priorities, it can help to make your intentions visual. For instance, you could map out the current allocation of resources across particular goals (perhaps as a pie chart?), and then invite the group to draw a new map or chart they'd like to be true three years from now. By having them do this task initially individually or in pairs then cascading to the full group, you might notice differences in aspiration that are worthy of further discussion. It can also help to inject targeted questions here, such as "Which of these achievements would have the greatest impact if everything else stayed the same?" or "Where are you spending your energy now and how might that have to shift in order to make these goals happen?" In this way, you can weight your priorities across the goals or objectives that you've now developed in your plan.

Once the performance standards have been identified, you can either list them within their own column in your plan or rewrite the goals or objectives with the measurements inserted. For example, if a previous objective had been to "increase member engagement," you may now be able to rewrite that objective as "increase membership by 35% over the next two years."

Goals	Measurable Objectives

Or

Goals	Objectives	Performance Standards

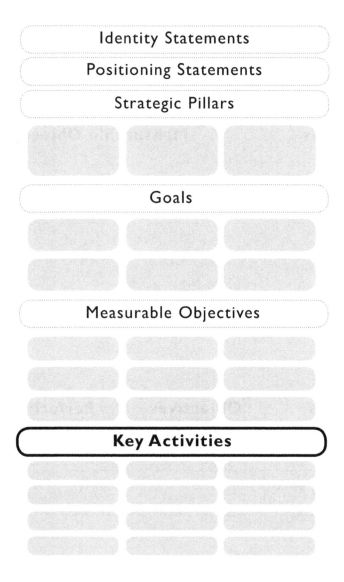

Strategic Plan Outline: Key Activities

- Positioning
- Strategic pillars
- Goals
- Objectives
- Performance standards
- Key activities

KEY ACTIVITIES

DELIVERABLE

The key activities or projects that will be undertaken within each objective.

Identifying key activities is particularly important in cases where those activities will require involvement and investment across organizational departments.

Some groups do not go to this level of operational detail in their strategic document. They invite their divisions or departmental leaders to identify activities within their individual operating plans instead. You can decide which approach will work best for your organization.

DECISION
___

Where to start.

Your key activities should not account for every single thing that will happen in order to accomplish every objective; rather, they are highlights: the first step, large projects, or the most important move that you're going to make within each area.

The identification of key activities is a good stage at which to invite a wider group of participants back into the planning process. Frontline staff are the ones most likely to know what to do and how to do it, and they are also the ones most likely to be implementing these activities. They will welcome a chance to be involved in crafting the plan at such a practical level. This step is critical not only for generating ideas but also for communicating the emerging content of your plan to the wider staff team.

To follow up on the example from the previous section:

If your objective is to increase membership by 35% in two years, possible key activities could include becoming more active on social media, merging with another association, initiating a professional development program, or hosting a world-class conference.

Note from this example the altitude of these activities. Many groups will have proposed activities such as these as objectives or even goals, but those higher-level elements should ideally stay focused on results. The activity level is where greater specificity comes in. It's your organizational to-do list.

KEY QUESTION
___

What do we most need to get busy doing?

___

HOW TO

Get 'er done.

To get at key activities, the focus question for your group is: "If our objective is X and our performance standard is Y, what must we do to get there?" Notice the "must we do" language. Your strategy document is not the place to list every possible thing you could do to move in a particular direction. The intent here is to identify the *key* activities that have to happen if the performance standards are to be met.

I often do this in stations around a room. Each table has the key question (as per above) for one objective, or a cluster of them. People are invited to write their suggestion of a key activity on a card and leave it on that table, then move around to the next table, and the next, until each table has been visited. By the end of the session, the tables will be covered with ideas for key activities.

You can then take a break and remove duplicates. I often write on one copy of a repeated idea how many people mentioned it, and/or I use a paper clip or staple to attach similar ideas to each other so that people's wording isn't lost.

Then I pull out the sticker dots! You may have experienced dotmocracy exercises before. A full treatment of them is beyond the scope of this book, but let me say this: I am not usually a fan. I only use dots when those dots have meaning. So the first step is to assign shared meaning to each color of dot. For example, if there are red, yellow, and green dots, we might agree that red means "Don't do it. It's an unadvisable idea." Green is "This idea is a must-do. I love it."[123] Yellow might mean "I am curious about this and would like to discuss it further." Alternatively, you can align the meaning of the dots with criteria you've previously set for an outstanding plan, such that, for instance, red means "innovative," blue means "impactful," and orange means "affordable." You then choose how many dots of each colour you give to each person, and they circulate around the tables spending their dots.[124]

The next stage is to interpret the data you've generated. If space and time allow, I often invite the whole group to gather around each table in turn to discuss what they notice about the input received. Perhaps you'll see all the dots clustered into just two or three ideas. Maybe some ideas have dots of only one colour. Some might have all three. What you're looking for are the high-leverage ideas that have a lot of dots representing positive attributes. If your dots are associated with different criteria, your best ideas will be the ones with a mixture of colors.

The next step is to alert the group to the fact that even now that the ideas have been assessed in this way, there are still a lot of them! So you facilitate a conversation about the criteria they would like the Steering Team to use when they decide which of the suggested activities should make it into the strategy. We're back again to the idea of what makes a good idea good. Even though the current group can't necessarily be around the table that makes the final decision, they can have confidence that they have given their ideas, ranked them collectively, and given some instructions to the team that's going to take the next step forward. That smaller team then collates all of that feedback to decide which key activities make it into the plan — usually one to three activities per objective.

You don't have to use dotmocracy. A simpler process to facilitate is to ask the group what the organization should stop, start, and continue doing to achieve the performance standards listed. (Dr. Jason Fox refers to this exercise as Stop/Start/Savvy Up, which I like even better!)[125] Another variation is to use two categories of activities: Dial Up and Dial Down. If the group is large, have them work in small groups to agree on ideas as a team — it will keep the volume of output more manageable. Once you have lists of possible options, you can follow a process similar to the one described above in order to help the Steering Team. The key to all these suggestions is that you can move from dozens of ideas to a handful of high-leverage ones.

"... fear and discomfort are an essential part of strategy making. In fact, if you are entirely comfortable with your strategy, there's a strong chance it isn't very good."

— Roger Martin —

• Quality check

QUALITY CHECK

DELIVERABLE

A process to ensure that the entire package up to this point matches and meets the criteria of success you've set.

This step does not yield a new component of the strategy, but rather offers an opportunity to fine-tune it to ensure it aligns with your organizational values and mission.

DECISION

Whether we're "done" enough to proceed.

As your plan takes shape, it will be easy to fall into the trap of simply wanting to get it done, or defending the choices you've made so far. Henry Mintzberg likens strategy to blinders on a horse — it's for keeping you on track, but it limits your peripheral vision.[126] Don't put those blinders on too soon! Instead, it's helpful to incorporate disciplined quality assurance at multiple points along the strategy-making way to offset that risk of tunnel vision. On page 65, I offered a general framework of six A's as high-level checks to remember as you develop your strategy. Now that you are at a stage where you need a more careful assessment, that list is expanded to a quality check framework of 14 elements. You may want to use all of them, or some of them, or even simply be inspired by them as you co-create a different list with your team.

Check these elements of your strategy:

1. **Altitude**. Make sure that all of the elements in a single section of the plan stay at a similar altitude. If a particular section is about high-level strategic issues, that's the level you're at all the way through; then when you move to sections dealing with mid-range issues or more detailed things, you stay at those more tactical levels throughout those sections. Your conversations will have dipped down into the weeds at ground level at times then veered back up again, but the final written iteration should be consistently strategic in each layer of the plan. Mintzberg affirms that "Effective strategists are not people who abstract themselves from the daily detail but quite the opposite: they are the ones who immerse themselves in it, while being able to abstract the strategic messages from it."[127] Be sure to communicate strategic messages and not daily details in each layer of the plan.

2. **Inspiration.** Is this plan exciting? Does it make you want to implement it? Does it make your palms sweat a little? Does it make you feel a bit tingly? The plan should light you up! It should be something you want to accomplish. Inspiration is a great quality check because your strategy might be beautifully aligned and look all spiffy with a nice, tidy series of tables, but if you don't actually want to do it and you can't imagine selling it as an idea to your supporters, staff or funders, then why bother?

3. **Impact.** If you implemented this plan, fully and well, would it make a great difference in the world? Would it actually have the impact that you want to make? Does it seem worth it? Sometimes, we can get so caught up in confirming the details that we lose sight of the reason we're doing it. As David Johnson suggests in his book

Trust, make sure you're not just doing the thing right, but doing the right thing.[128] Your strategy should move you significantly forward toward achieving your mission. Make sure it does.

4. **Clarity.** Your plan should be communicated in language that makes sense to people. Consider how your audiences speak and think. Understanding your strategy should not be predicated on having attended every planning meeting; it should be compelling and clear on its own. It shouldn't be full of code, acronyms, or jargon, and it shouldn't make reference to previous conversations, especially those of which not everyone was a part.

5. **Vertical alignment.** Your high-level elements should cascade through your mid-range elements to your detailed elements (and back again). The idea is that if you handle all the details, that will lead to accomplishing the mid-range objectives, and if you accomplish those mid-range objectives, that in turn will lead to achieving your high-level goals. Your strategy will inevitably have unintended consequences, both positive and negative, but the key here is to scan the plan vertically to ensure it is likely to have an aligned, cascading effect.

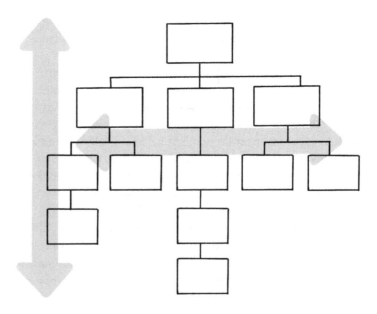

6. **Comprehensiveness.** Your plan should capture the full scope of what your organization does, assuming that was your intention in the first place. Are there big parts of your organization not represented here? Sometimes people can get distracted by new, shiny priorities and forget to think about the overall organizational strategy for the core business.

7. **Accuracy.** Ask challenging questions that pressure test the accuracy of the assumptions on which your strategy is based. What if the opposite were actually true? Ask disconfirming questions, such as what problems your strategy will create or leave unsolved. Your strategy should be able to withstand this level of internal critique before heading out into the world.

8. **Relevance.** Does your strategy respond to the relevant trends and other environmental factors you identified in the early stages of your planning? Too often organizations go to great pains to describe their context, but never actually adapt their decisions accordingly. Depending on how long you've been developing your plan, there's also the chance that key features of your context have shifted in the meantime. Review your context and make sure your strategy still resonates.

9. **People.** Does this strategy lead you to benefit the people you most want to serve? (It is also helpful to ask whether you have the right people on your team to accomplish that level of service, but we'll come to capacity assessments soon. For now, ensure your strategy is taking you in the right direction). Would accomplishing it move you closer to meeting the needs of your customers or clients?

10. **Reach.** Some organizations set "moonshot" strategies, so named to reflect the lofty American ambition of getting to the moon by the end of the decade in the 1960s. Other strategies are more modest, reaching only slightly beyond the current vision, and others still find themselves somewhere in between. Either can be effective. As a quality check, develop a shared sense of where on this spectrum your current strategy falls overall. Then, within that, you may identify elements that fall into the opposite category. This is the appropriate time to check your level of ambitiousness and to develop a shared understanding of the relative level of courage that will be needed to succeed within each goal area.

"The eye sees only
what the mind is prepared to comprehend."
&— Robertson Davies —&

11. **Strategic-ness**. It's easy to get caught in the trap of thinking that the most efficient, easily implementable plan is necessarily the best one. Parts of your strategic plan can end up reading like a to-do list that you could handle over a few days if you gave it some concerted attention. I admittedly enjoy writing things on my to-do list just to have the pleasure of crossing them off. This approach gives you a sense of meaningful progress but may not actually be meaningful at all. Even an intentionally modest strategy should not be one you can achieve in 10% of the allotted time, practically with your eyes closed. Success is no doubt motivating, but if you include "low-hanging fruit" or "quick wins" in your strategy, make sure they are in fact impactful moves and not just an excuse to clear your tactical backlog under the guise of making truly strategic progress.

12. **Theoretical framework**. By this, I mean two related things: What worldview or strategic understanding does your strategy espouse (implicitly or explicitly), and does it operate in line with your theory of change? In *Strategy Safari,* Mintzberg, Ahlstrand, and Lampel list a variety of issues that cut across and differentiate the schools of thought in strategy making.[129] These issues include who gets to act as the strategist, how fixed or emergent your strategy is, how generic or customized, how stable or predictable it assumes the world to be, and how strategy balances thinking and acting. Your organization's values, politics, and understanding of the world should be reflected in all aspects of your strategic process.

13. **Palette.** This check is all about language. If in one section of your plan you have 10 steps toward something, you want to make sure that each of those steps is phrased similarly. If some of them start with a verb, they should all start with a verb. If some start with a noun, they should all start with a noun. This is an editing step to make sure that the linguistic palette of your strategy (i.e. verb tenses, choice of language, consistency of terminology) supports rather than distracts from your message.

14. **Definition of done.** Three years from now, would you be able to assess your organization's results against this strategy and emerge with a clear sense of how close you came to achieving it? More

importantly, how likely would it be that several of your colleagues would draw the same conclusion from the same body of evidence?

Other criteria of success can be applied only once you have begun implementing the strategy. Lafley and Martin suggest various markers, several of which are perhaps more applicable to the private sector than to the social sector. Examples include having more resources to spend than your competitors, customers who look to you first for innovation, competitors who are attacking others more than they are attacking you, and "customers who absolutely adore you, and non-customers who can't see why anybody would buy from you"[130] We will return to this concept in a later section on monitoring. For now, I mention it to highlight that achieving the performance standards set out in your plan may not go far enough in telling you whether you developed a worthwhile plan in the first place.

KEY QUESTION

Is this a good strategy?

HOW TO

Check-ins.

Assessment of your strategy can happen both formally and informally throughout its development.

Formally, you may wish to insert an assessment phase at this point, where you invite broader input into the draft strategy as a whole. In real life, what this often looks like is pulling together the various components that have been developed through the steps outlined above and circulating them, with some prompting questions, to a circle of advisors. That circle might include other members of your board of directors, other senior staff, or perhaps a couple of trusted, wise counselors from outside of your organization.

You may also choose to do this at several points throughout your strategy development process. Just be sure that the questions you ask your reviewers match the stage that you're at. If you're asking questions early, you might ask, "What advice do you have for us as we think about planning?"

If you're seeking feedback later, once you have a draft in hand, the questions should be oriented toward validation or refinement, for example, "Does this strategy reflect your understanding of what our organization should be about?" or "Do you see any glaring omissions or errors?" It's the difference between writing a book and editing it. Ask clearly for the kind of feedback you most need at this stage.

You could use the 14 criteria provided above as your starting point. You could ask reviewers to score your draft of the strategy on a scale of one to ten against each of those criteria, for example.

Informal feedback is harder to gather for strategy making if the process has comprised a series of workshops or conversations to which only selected people were invited. In this case, you need to give people in your organization enough information to be able to make informed judgements before you actively solicit their input. It may not be enough to invite them to make suggestions if you haven't given them enough fodder to inform their observations. Strategy expert Alicia McKay refers to this as creating meaning before issuing instructions. In a sense, the informal assessment channels depend on the formal ones.[131] That's why having a thorough and frequent communication plan throughout your strategy development process is so important.

Too often people involve a broad range of stakeholders in the environmental scanning phase early on, then present them with a plan at the end, without offering any opportunities for involvement in between. If you can insert such opportunities throughout the process to elicit input, your plan will generate greater buy-in. As Dr. Max Mckeown says, "If they don't believe in it, they won't act on it."[132]

One way of doing this is to invite a wider group of stakeholders to weigh in on particular strategic challenges as they arise. Earlier I referred to these as knots that needed to be untangled. I have found it helpful to alert staff or other stakeholders to some of those knots — the sticky points the group has been wrestling with — and give them a specific opportunity to weigh in on those. This allows you to both increase people's sense of ownership over the plan and elicit their wisdom in getting some of these strategic knots untangled.

Another approach is to involve people in deciding on resource allocation. You can do this in a fun and tactile way using beads, poker chips, Monopoly money, or some other currency. You give people a limited amount of currency to be spent on a range of priorities, and invite them to choose how to spend that currency. This exercise not only helps you understand where their priorities lie, but also helps them appreciate how difficult it is to make decisions amongst worthwhile and compelling options. (As an added bonus, you could add an activity where they can provide ideas as to how to get more currency!)

Not only can assessment be formal or informal, it can also be structured or unstructured. That is, you can provide a clear set of principles or a rubric against which to assess the strategy as it evolves, or you can simply ask people for their comments. Be clear on whether you are interested in receiving open-ended feedback or input on a more closed set of options.

This is where decision rights become particularly important. There are plenty of opportunities to ask for input along the way, but at some point, decisions about the final strategy need to be made. Communicate those alongside a rationale for how and why you have chosen to move in that direction. If a broader group of stakeholders has been aware of some of the dilemmas you've faced and has had some voice in addressing them, they are more likely to be accepting of the solutions that are being proposed.[133]

In trying to simplify the process here for ease of presentation, I fear I have made it appear more linear than it really is in practice. To be clear: assessment should happen throughout your strategy-making process, in a feedback loop of iterating, getting feedback, revising, and going back again.

You may find that the results of your assessment compel you to circle back to the **Attune** or **Align** phases of strategy making. If you are satisfied that your strategy is "done enough," you can carry on to the **Adapt** phase.

ANTICIPATE   ATTUNE   ALIGN   ASSESS   **ADAPT**   ARCHIVE

- Capacity analysis
- Implementation plan
- Execution systems
- Monitoring plan

A strategy's value is heavily tied to our ability to make it happen, because only then will it have its intended impact on the world (often alongside many other impacts we did not anticipate!).

Whenever a group gets to the chronological planning portion of a multi-year strategy, it's not surprising to find that year one is full of detail, year two is considerably less so, and year three has hardly anything written in it. We can't envision details very far in advance. We can more easily predict what it's going to take to get things done in the short term than in the longer term. We also know that we are prone to overestimating what we can do in the short term and underestimating what we can do in the long term.

I'm conscious that the arc of this book follows a similar pattern. I can provide more details about the earlier steps of the strategy making process than I can about the later steps. This section on adaptation has less detail in it, for two main reasons. First, because it is often an internal process. As much as I am privy to parts of it, I am not internal to any organization and so I don't have a front row seat to observe or facilitate these steps the way I often do at earlier stages. Second, the further down the strategy making road you go, the more divergent paths there are, and therefore my ability to anticipate the specific instructions you will need is more limited. It reminds me of parenting. When our children were little, most of our friends parented very similarly to us. But as the kids hit middle school, and certainly as they moved into high school, our parenting approaches began to diverge quite noticeably. There were more variables and variation to take into account. As a result, we felt more tentative in our ability to describe how to do it well. I have a similar feeling now. I'll therefore outline the steps that need to happen and point you to resources written by authors who specialize in the execution of plans.

This stage is about adaptation — adapting your organization's way of doing things to align with the strategic intentions you've set. It's where the "stickiness" of your strategy is determined — in real life where things actually happen or they don't.

CAPACITY ANALYSIS

DELIVERABLE

An assessment of what it will take to get this plan done.

This is where you measure your plan against your current capabilities, competencies, and resources. This step can occur informally or formally. You don't want to do this at the beginning of the process, because it would lead you to a status quo kind of plan. It's much better to map out where you want to go and then later figure out what you need to get there. By then you'll have a clearer sense of how strongly committed you are to your path forward. And virtually anything is achievable with sufficient resources invested in it! So, this is the stage of planning where you take stock of your skills, your systems, your habits, and your mindsets to see what you'll need to do or acquire to get where you're going.

DECISION

What it will take to execute this strategy.

This is the time to have conversations about "what will it take" versus "whatever it takes." Achieving your strategy might mean doing things you haven't done before. Or doing things faster or differently. Maybe it means dropping some things to free up space to do what you've committed to doing. Your investment priorities may need to shift. This is the time to assess how far you are from where you want to be in terms of your ability to implement this plan.

In general, your decisions here will take one of two broad forms: "If we are committed to this strategy, we need to find the resources to support it," or "Now that we've had a sober second look, we need to adjust our objectives or targets to fall more realistically in line with the resources we are likely to have available."

KEY QUESTION

Do we have what it takes?

———

HOW TO

What it will require.

This step usually happens in tandem with implementation planning. And to the extent that your strategy making has built on your strengths, affirmed your mission, and identified what you will do less of, you are likely to find that you already possess much of what it will take to get there.

You can choose to analyze your organization's capacity systematically or organically. The former is more structured, often using an external assessment tool. The latter is more emergent, addressing capacity gaps intuitively in advance, or as they arise in the course of implementation.

If you opt for systematic analysis, you may choose to use one of the many proven organizational capacity assessment (OCA) tools already available, or you can develop your own. OCA tools are often used for accreditation purposes and may include very general questions such as "Does your organization have a mission statement? A strategic plan? Monitoring systems in place?" These tools may prove to be more useful for general and generic assessments than for a specific analysis of your capacity to implement your plan at this time. You may, however, find you can borrow selected questions or measurements to suit your purpose. You can then align them with the pillars of your strategy as you do a gap analysis of where you are now versus where you hope to be.

If you opt for a more emergent approach, you will fill capacity gaps as they arise rather than trying to anticipate in advance what they will be. You will likely carry on with generic investments in human capital, for example, such as progressive policies, hiring practices, and professional development, trusting that your strong, well-equipped team will figure out what they need to have, know, and do as they go along.

Most organizations locate themselves somewhere in the middle. Leaders have probably already become aware of prospective gaps, through the strategy making process itself and through conversations with their team. Filling those gaps — through investing in hiring, organizational structure redesign, training, technology, etc. — is likely to happen concurrently with or early in strategy implementation. Costing happens in broad strokes and is delegated to, then aggregated from, division- or department-level operational planning.

The mechanics are less critical than ensuring this step happens. Too often, new strategic directions are added onto existing expectations, resulting in tired, distracted staff, shallow commitment, and weak implementation.

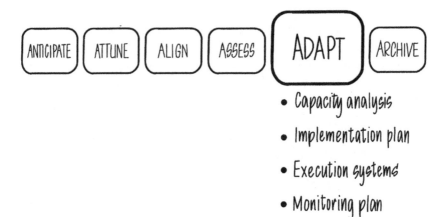

- Capacity analysis
- Implementation plan
- Execution systems
- Monitoring plan

IMPLEMENTATION PLAN

DELIVERABLE

A clear sense of who is doing what by when, in order to achieve your performance standards in the short and the longer term.

Developing the implementation plan provides another reality check on the strategy and helps people across the organization visualize the interdependencies inherent in the plan.

DECISION

How to get 'er done.

In *The 4 Disciplines of Execution,* McChesney and Covey describe implementation as "says easy, does hard."[134] Many people make reference to implementation as if it is a foregone conclusion, but it is enormously difficult to achieve in real life. How implementation is planned can contribute to the likelihood of it happening.

The implementation planning stage is often where you see people rolling their eyes or zoning out at the end of a meeting. They look at their phones and avoid making eye contact as the facilitator at the front of the room says, "So, who wants to sign up for task A, or B, or C?" That's not what I have in mind for the implementation planning phase of your strategy. It is an opportunity to reinforce strategic priorities and to inspire commitment through continued engagement.

Particularly now, as planning timeframes are shortening and lengthening at the same time, we want to take a long view and make sure our plans are moving in the right direction. But we can only do that in a detailed way for the initial few steps. Edgar Schein talks about this in *Humble Consulting,* asserting the value of making "the next small adaptive move."[135] Dr. Jason Fox, in *How to Lead a Quest,* also talks about shining a light on the next step in front of us. With each step comes a new vantage point; what we can see looks different again... and so we plan one step at a time.[136] I recommend using an emergent strategy, that is, one step at a time, while also maintaining a longer sightline to make sure that those steps are ultimately taking you in the direction you want to go. As the saying goes, "We make the path by walking."[137]

At the same time, leaders need to devote particular energy and diligence to the "wildly important" because not all tasks are equal.[138] McChesney and Covey liken this to being an air traffic controller who sees the whole sky, but lands one plane at a time. Cowley and Domb refer to it as "pushing on one big boulder at a time."[139] Implementation planning is an opportunity for prioritization and for modelling calm, focused leadership.

KEY QUESTION

Specifically, who's doing what when?

HOW TO

Once again, define "done".

Implementation planning can be as simple as mapping out the components of your key activities onto a calendar in sequence, with the names of the people responsible attached. Those components should be framed as tasks, for as James Clear says, specific tasks are the difference between our desires and our results.[140] If we only think about what we want, we're likely to get lukewarm results, but if we commit to doing something specific, we are much more likely to get it done.[141]

Implementation planning template

Task	Definition of Done/ Success	Deadline/ Timeframe	Person Responsible	Critical Success Factors

You're probably familiar with Gantt charts, which are a useful tool for scheduling projects. To take your typical Gantt chart one step further, add a column for a co-created definition of done. It helps to create a deliberate and explicit mental model of each task at hand, just like you did at the start of your strategy making process.

Imagine you're sitting in an event meeting planning and someone says, "I'll take care of communications." If I were to ask you to describe what you think that person has volunteered to take on, your answer could legitimately range from "She's going to manage our social media feed" to "She's going to write some press releases and circulate a digital poster" or even "She's going to do a full-scale communications strategy, including hiring a marketing agency and building our public relations capacity over the next two years." Likewise for all the other participants in the room. Without a conversation about how these various interpretations measure up against the volunteer's actual intention, it's quite possible that people's expectations around the table will not be met.

The same is true for all parts of strategy implementation. You need to be very clear about who's responsible for what by when, but also to make sure that your team has a shared definition of done. If "done" is not the appropriate descriptor for your task at hand, perhaps you can at least do what Dr. Max Mckeown describes as "translating the strategy into five to seven principles that clearly indicate the kind of behaviour that is needed to succeed." [142]

Another implementation planning possibility is to create a bullseye-style diagram for each key activity in your plan, where the layers represent different levels of commitment. Participants then sign up for the level of involvement they want in each activity, and there you have it: ready-made project teams.

This exercise is essentially a self-selection process. People making their own commitments is often an advantage, but may not be universally applicable. Another advantage is that it allows you and the whole group to see which activities have generated considerable enthusiasm and which are lacking. What you choose to do with that information may range from making a decision to exclude that activity

or objective because it is simply not seen as exciting or high priority for your team, through to shoring up your capacity in that area
because no one around your current table has the interest, time, or
mandate to take it on.

You can see that engagement in both of these implementation planning activities is a learning opportunity in itself. The process can be
as valuable as the product, even in something as tactical as implementation planning.

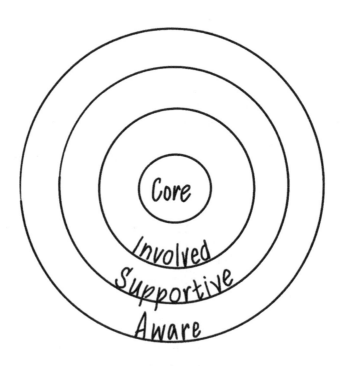

"The chains of habit
are too weak to be felt
until they are too strong to be broken."
— Samuel Johnson —

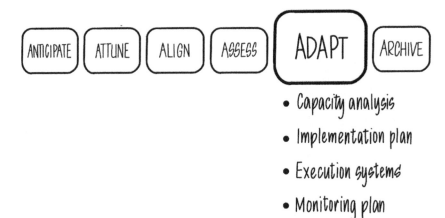

- Capacity analysis
- Implementation plan
- Execution systems
- Monitoring plan

EXECUTION SYSTEMS

DELIVERABLE

Systems to turn your strategic intentions into actions and results.

This component is unlikely to find its way into your written strategic plan, but your plan is guaranteed to flounder without it. Effective organizational systems are essential if you are to turn your strategic intentions into a reality.

DECISION

How to stick with it.

Let's talk about how to make your strategy stick so it truly gathers momentum and not dust. Plans don't do that — systems do. As

James Clear notes, "Goals are good for planning your progress and systems are good for actually making progress."[143] But it is also true that those same systems can impede your progress and undermine the effectiveness of your plan.

It's one thing to know where you're heading. It's quite another to get there. Getting there requires not just an implementation plan, but actual execution! Repeated actions that allow you, little by little, to make progress over time, toward the destination you've identified as being worthy of your attention. This is where you actually start paying the cost that you decided earlier you were willing to pay, in order to achieve your aspirations. As Technology of Participation (ToP) Facilitator Jo Nelson says, "History doesn't change from the big things that you ought to do. History changes from the little things you actually do."[144]

You need to embed your strategic priorities into the habits of your workplace. When you are developing systems for achieving your goals, if you can attach or embed implementation practices into things you are already doing unconsciously, those goals are much more likely to happen. Clear calls this "habit stacking." For instance, if an Executive Director or CEO is already making a report to her board each month, she can tweak that report format so that its categories align with the structure and standards of the strategy. Or if she receives an automated notification each time her organization receives a donation, she can design a habit of sending a thank you message to that donor as soon as she receives the notification, thereby advancing her objective related to donor appreciation. When you create a system of habits that support you toward your goals, no one has to wonder, "Am I staying aligned with the strategic plan?" Your accountability systems guarantee it.

We are also more likely to be successful if we align our environment with our goals. This is true at a micro level: someone who sets their running shoes right by their bed at night is more likely to put those shoes on in the morning and go for a run than someone who has to dig through the closet to find them. But it's also true at higher organizational levels. As Edgar Schein says, "an organization can only do what is compatible with its culture."[145] If your organizational culture is out of alignment with the goals you've set, the likelihood that you will consistently achieve those goals is low. When you're constantly pushing against the prevailing culture, change is much more difficult than if you're able to shift that culture over time to be supportive of your goals. Find ways to swim with the current rather than against it.

Another way to embed your strategy is in your communications. Make your plan simple, and memorable, then put the highlights of it on repeat so people hear it over and over again.   Be sure to communicate examples of how the plan is working. Demonstrate that you have made decisions to say yes or no to certain things based on the priorities it contains. Explain how the strategy has allowed you to make progress toward the goals that you've set. Help your team to see that having the plan has been useful in achieving the impact you hoped it would. Similarly, communicate examples of pivoting in response to changing conditions and show that doing so does not suggest that the strategy is not worthwhile. Rather, it shows you that you had a direction and made a conscious choice to deviate from it for particular, defensible reasons.

These principles apply at broad cultural and communication levels, but are also relevant to the work habits of individuals. We see this with writers who set themselves a word goal per hour instead of per day, or people who use the Pomodoro time management technique to see how much they can get done in just 25 minutes, or those who write things on their to-do list in order to cross them off. The feeling of making progress leads to more progress. So break down individual responsibilities within the strategy into specific, manageable chunks. Just as a flywheel can be hard to get started but then gradually builds on its own momentum, a small initial investment of willpower and discipline will set you up for long-term motivation and results. Once you've built something into a habit, it can continue at an unconscious level on its own momentum. It's true for your personal exercise regime, and it's also true for your organization's strategic goals.

KEY QUESTION

**What habits do we need to develop?**

HOW TO

Stacking.

Now's the time to identify categories of actions within which you want your plan to stick. You can do this as a group for corporate areas, or individually for personal ones.

Make a table of three columns, and write these categories in the first column. As shown in the example below, these might include "Reporting to the board," "Incentive system," "Communication to staff," and "Individual time management." You could also add "Hiring practices," "Professional development investment," or "Fundraising activities" — any elements where you would like to see evidence of your strategy making a difference and where you would like to experience more ease.

In the second column, note what your current practice is.

In the third, indicate how you could tweak that habit to align more closely with the strategy. Think in terms of making a handful of key decisions that make dozens or even hundreds of other decisions unnecesary.[146]

Actions	Current Practice	Tweak needed
Reporting to the board		
Incentive system		
Communication to staff		
Individual time management		

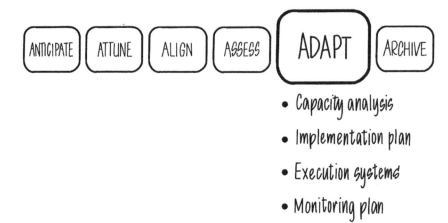

- Capacity analysis
- Implementation plan
- Execution systems
- Monitoring plan

MONITORING PLAN

DELIVERABLE

A plan for assessing how well you are staying on track.

The output of this step is more of a rhythm than a written document. It reflects your organizational discipline in reviewing how well your plan is serving you. Monitoring should assess two primary elements: are the strategic activities happening, and are they working. This cadence of review usually relies on something visual — a dashboard or a scorecard — to capture how you're doing.

DECISION

How to know whether the strategy is happening and working.

Your strategy is designed to be a tool to help you. There is no strategic planning cop that's going to show up and say, "But you said you would do it this way!" Your monitoring plan should therefore feel helpful to you as both a guardrail and a tailwind keeping you moving forward, not as handcuffs that keep you attached to a plan that no longer makes sense. It's designed to keep your sightline clear.

Decisions should not be revisited simply because we forgot we made them in the first place. This will only lead us to have the same conversations over and over again, like a hamster on a wheel, rather than actually making forward progress. Each time a decision is made, I think of it as a gate being closed behind us as we continue moving forward. But that's not to say that you can never cycle back and unlock those gates. Part of what builds momentum is having a cadence of review, a known rhythm for monitoring how things are going with your plan. That quality check starts with the big-picture metrics you've developed at a strategic level and should cascade through to more detailed monitoring of departmental or activity-based metrics. In *The 4 Disciplines of Execution*, McChesney and Covey underscore the importance of regularity and rhythm in supporting execution of previous strategy decisions.[147] A simple way to do this is to agree that decisions will be piloted now and revisited in six months' time.

But it also helps to make explicit any other conditions under which decisions should be revisited.[148] For instance, you may agree that you will revisit decisions if the conditions under which they were made have dramatically changed. So, if something in your context changes quite significantly (such as a global pandemic, perhaps?), then it makes sense to reconsider your plan. When your team knows that decisions will be opened for discussion under certain future conditions, they will be less tempted to re-open them sooner than that.

Inevitably, some portions of your strategy will be successfully achieved and others will remain unrealized. Alongside those, unintended or unanticipated results will also surface. Henry Mintzberg highlights the importance of combining both projected and emergent results as you monitor your strategy's success.[149] He also reminds us of the need for humility, asserting that "a kind of normative naivete has pervaded the literature of planning — confident beliefs in what is best, grounded in an ignorance of what really does work!"[150] Dr. Max Mckeown emphasizes the need for agility and flexibility in enacting a strategic plan: "Any fool can produce a plan. The genius is in seeing how new events open up new possibilities for the old plan. Or even entirely new plans that weren't possible when the old plan was written." Your greatest strategic success may come from strategic responses to unplanned opportunities.

Your plan should be a generative one, such that you are able to respond to changing conditions while also creating conditions that give your plan even greater traction. One board I know that is committed to generative governance has each individual board member set a personal goal at the start of each year. One director assigned herself the task of asking generative questions at every monthly meeting, thereby pushing that board into new territory, into greater creativity, into deeper reflection. Your strategy should serve a similar purpose for you. People should be doing what it says not because the strategy says so, but because it has that compelling missional quality that makes people want to do it. If your strategy is capturing what you wanted to do anyway — the kind of people you want in your team, the kind of organization you want to grow into becoming — you'll be enacting it because it is compelling, aligned, and the right thing to do, not simply because you said you would.

Monitoring is a learning tool that allows us to be systematically flexible. It's an exercise both of "doing things right" and "doing the right things." As Dr. Max Mckeown says, "Getting the wrong thing done well is still the wrong thing."[151] Advice in the literature on setting habits that stick, by writers such as James Clear, Charles Duhigg, and B. J. Fogg, suggests that rather than looking ahead to where you want to be five years from now, you should look at where you were very recently, and get slightly better. For example, look at your time management or your feedback to your team from last week and

"You can't place your hope on distant goals or objectives... because you don't know what the future holds and if they will even be relevant then. You don't have the answers. And so, instead of squinting into the future, you need to shine a light on the path in front of us, and celebrate small wins along the way."

— Dr. Jason Fox —

get one percent better at those specific things this week, because achieving tiny milestones builds momentum.[152]

Yet at the same time, we need to make sure that we are making those one percent improvements in the right long-term direction, based both on our original intentions and iteratively as conditions change, toward impacts that matter. So it's putting one foot in front of the other, while checking to ensure you're on the right path in the first place.

KEY QUESTION

How are we doing and how do we know?

HOW TO

Systematically flexible.

Your monitoring system should be simple and compelling. One straightforward design is to develop and document a four-part process:

1. Rhythm
2. Reconnaissance
3. Results
4. Reporting

1. **Rhythm** – How often will your plan be reviewed, under what conditions, and by whom? The criteria of success should be based around the performance standards within the plan itself but should also incorporate a "relevance check" to ensure alignment with your broader context.

2. **Reconnaissance** – What systems do you have in place for tracking and interpreting relevant changes in your context that affect your strategy? How often do you lift your gaze and look around? How thorough and well curated is your information diet? For many organizations, this reconnaissance function could be a key role played by the board of directors, but it is unfortunately often underperformed.

3. **Results** – How will you capture your progress? A useful tool for this is a dashboard or scorecard that visually represents your progress against key standards or milestones that are meaningful to your audience(s), drawn from your full strategy. As McChesney and Covey assert, "The scoreboard should be created by the players, not the coach."[153] It also helps to include a section on your dashboard for capturing unintended or emergent results in addition to those that were deliberately achieved.

4. **Reporting** – One difference between casually golfing with your friends on a weekend and playing in a professional tournament (in addition to the quality of the play!) is how the score is kept. I can only imagine that television ratings would plummet if there were no leaderboard or commentators, and players simply tracked their scores individually and stuck their scorecard into their back pocket before continuing to the next hole. Winning drives morale and engagement. Be sure you are not only tracking your results but communicating them in an appealing way to those who care about them. The democratization of monitoring – doing it together and reviewing it together – is a powerful way to build trust and buy-in.

And don't forget to celebrate! Because strategy making is often an iterative process, it can feel endless. We have a tendency to celebrate endings but ignore the smaller wins inside ongoing processes. Consider creating milestones and markers that are worthy of appreciation along the way. Celebrate every win.

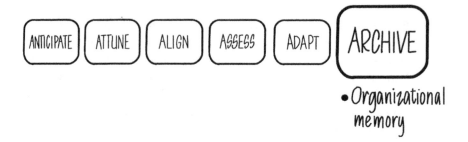

•Organizational
memory

ORGANIZATIONAL MEMORY

DELIVERABLE

Organizational memory: a collection of data, information, and knowledge generated by and about your organization.

Developing organizational memory means documenting the steps followed, the decisions made, and the outputs generated over time for future reference or use. The results of this component should be generated throughout the planning process, and are summarized and catalogued at the end.

DECISION

How to capture the strategy-making process for future reference.

When a strategic plan sits on a shelf gathering dust, it's rarely the fault of the plan itself. It could be because the plan has not been communicated in a way that is memorable or evocative or relevant for people, and therefore it has not been embedded in their routines and reward systems. In my experience, the plans that get used most are about two pages long, not twenty.

Nevertheless, it is helpful to have a much more comprehensive suite of documents that captures the process by which that plan was developed in the first place. That package serves not as frequent reading material but as organizational memory, so that as you drift away from the plan, or when you want to develop a new one three to five years down the road, you can refer to it and recall what you did and why. This set of documents should describe what you did and how those methodological choices unfolded, what you heard, what you decided, and why. It is both objective and reflective. It makes your logic explicit and keeps a record of what you said yes and no to. When you come to repeat the process, this will help you determine which parts worked well and which parts did not serve you well.

I have no illusions that these longer reports are going to be read in great detail by many people. They really aren't designed for that. They aren't intended for public relations or staff communication or catchy summaries that roll off the tongue. They are for archiving what happened in the organization so that you can go back to it later as needed.

It is common for people to rely too heavily on summary documents. As time goes on, the meanings assigned to particular labels or activities can stray from their original intentions. It is therefore immensely helpful to have a place that you can go back to and say, "No, actually when we said that we meant this, not this other thing, and I think we're a little bit off course." Consulting the archive may only happen right at the end of the planning cycle, when you're ready to go and do this whole thing again, or it may happen at multiple points along the way. The important thing is, it's there whenever you need guidance and reminders.

This level of detail is also helpful to guide implementation. When you are six to 18 months into implementing a plan, you can go back to some of the materials that were too tactical to find their way into the original strategic plan, but were kept on file for later use.

As the execution of your plan progresses, it is helpful to have those operational suggestions well organized and documented for reference as you need them.

KEY QUESTION

What did we decide and why?

———

HOW TO

———

Methodology, rationale, and reflections.

Documentation of the strategy-making process happens in three phases: as you go along, at the submission of polished deliverables, and upon final reflection.

The format of this documentation will likely vary over time as your preferred means of capturing organizational memory change with technology and preferences. It could be a document, a slide deck, a voice recording, a series of links, or any number of other formats. What's important is that you do keep track, in whatever way makes most sense to you.

Be intentional about documenting the strategy-making process as you go along. You think you'll remember the nuances later, but you won't. You then end up with a process document that emerged as the strategy-making project evolved.

When the process is complete, your polished set of final deliverables serves as core documentation. Perhaps this is the package that goes to the board.

After that, in the spirit of finishing well, you may also choose to make sure that your suite of documents contains an overall reflection on the process of creating your strategic plan. This is something that simply can't be captured until the whole thing is done. Capturing this snapshot explicitly and intentionally will be a gift to your future self.

WRAP-UP

Finishing well

Wrap-up

This is a book that holds various concepts in tension. I find that living right in the middle of polarities is a generative place to be.

So we find ourselves in the middle. In the middle between leading decisively and listening to input. Between having a firm destination and being flexible about how to get there. Between leading courageously and being humble about our ability to predict the future. We are also in the middle of the balance between process and product. The book takes us deep into details while providing high-level justification for investment in this kind of work. It straddles the two worlds of the leader who wants to hire someone to help them develop their strategic plan and the leader who wants or needs to navigate that process themselves. In either case, may you be an ambassador for strategy making that happens both out loud and on purpose.

When the context is uncertain, it can be too easy to retrench. To become passive, or silent, or nostalgic to the point of irrelevance. We know that now more than ever. Stay strong. Because to the extent that leaders can cast a compelling vision of the future and map a path to get there, guided by a sense of both certainty and adventure, we all benefit.

I started by discussing the benefits of collaborative strategic planning. Collaborative processes reduce blind spots and increase buy-in. Done well, they can also increase our bravery. It is my sincere hope that as collaborative leadership becomes the default setting for most organizations, we will push our collaborative planning to the next frontier: collaboration first across agencies and then across sectors, for the benefit of a broader system or community. One of the responsibilities of being a director on a board is that you are a steward of the success of that organization. It is your highest calling in that role. The irony is that when it comes to strategy making, sometimes you are faced with a dilemma: what is good for your organization alone may not in fact be good for the achievement of its wider mission, which is often to benefit citizens of the wider community. If forced to choose, which do you uphold? When we have directors who conceive of their role in its larger sense, seeing themselves as guardians of their organizational mission rather than as protectors of the forms, preferences, and territories of the organization itself, we're more likely to move toward a situation where collaborative planning occurs not just across silos inside one organization, but across that broader community for the greater good.

As I finish writing this book, I am four months into sheltering at home due to the COVID-19 global pandemic. I have no idea where you will be in that story when you read it. My hope is that COVID-19 will be a distant memory for all of us by then. But if there's one positive to come out of all this, it's that COVID-19 has injected a sense of urgency to our collaboration that has led to some ingenious and generous collective efforts that are going to benefit many people for many years. I think of organizations that have been able to break down the barriers between sectors that have traditionally worked separately, such as emergency shelters and healthcare. I think of a private sector company that decided to make its proprietary specifications for ventilators open source so that creative teams of clever people could build on their expertise and make medical equipment more accessible, to more people, faster. I think of thriving new organizations that are employing at-risk youth, organizations that did not exist even as an idea before this pandemic hit. I think of neighbors and neighborhoods that are building new relationships and connections, even in the midst of isolation. The same might be true in some families.

It seems like a strange time to be thinking about strategy making, when we can barely see around the next bend. Can we really write the ending from the middle of a story? I would argue that now more than ever is the time to forge a clear sightline toward the kinds of communities we want to build, even when our familiar ways of doing so are being turned upside down. The most effective organizations and leaders I know right now are those that are willing to stay true to their "why" while maintaining a very loose grip on the "how."

This is the nimble and strategic leadership that's needed now. It's an ongoing habit, not an event.[154]

I trust that this book will continue to be a valued resource for you as we all emerge from an event that will forever mark our generation. Most of us have never lived through something of this magnitude before, and we're doing it together, at a global scale. One of the pearls emerging from this gritty experience is the truly shared nature of it. It is certainly my hope that we will take the best of what we're learning out of this chapter and into the next one. It will be those who can lead with a magical combination of certainty and flexibility who will take us there.

Here´s our team

Dr. Rebecca Sutherns

I am an expert in collaborative planning. I provide strategic coaching, group facilitation, training, and governance support to CEOs and Boards of Directors. I have been bringing intellect, enthusiasm, and varied experience to my working mission-driven leaders around the world for more than 20 years, helping them achieve strategic clarity, spend their time well, and make wiser decisions faster. I run programs that are nimbly facilitated, and I can teach you and your team to do the same.

Visit rebeccasutherns.com to learn more, including about my first book: *Nimble: Off Script But Still On Track — A coaching guide for responsive facilitation.*

I'd welcome hearing from you if you're interested in working together.

+1 519 994 0064
rebecca@rebeccasutherns.com
LinkedIn: rebeccasutherns
Twitter: @RebeccaSutherns

Laurie Watson

Laurie Watson is Rebecca's Business Manager and provides project management expertise and administrative support on a variety of projects. She is a highly skilled, detail-oriented communications professional with strong organizational skills. Laurie is a fast learner with a wide range of practical skills and an appreciation for good grammar.

Rosanna von Sacken

Rosanna von Sacken, M.Sc., CPF, is the founder and principal consultant of Advanced Consulting and Facilitation Ltd., based in metro Vancouver, B.C., Canada (www.advancedconsultingfacilitation.com). She has been working with groups and organizations of various sizes in all sectors as a visual facilitator, a visual coach, and as an emergency management consultant for over 20 years. Rosanna also uses her creative and lettering skills to draw and create explainer videos, both of which complement her facilitation and consulting work. Find her @rosanna_acf on social media.

Oliver Sutherns

Oliver Sutherns brings a unique blend of creativity, logic, and intelligence to the design table. He has a passion for solving problems and making things work. Building on the philosophy that there is no design without function, and that in everything there is a little art, Oliver seeks to consistently find that elusive space between design and function that gives a project life. www.oliversutherns.com

Hambone Publishing

Hambone Publishing is a boutique publishing company based in Melbourne, Australia. Started by sister and brother duo Michelle and Ben Phillips, they help authors with all stages of publishing a book. They have particular experience and interest in books written by thought leaders (due to a desire to be continuously learning) and healthcare (due to their mother's passion for spreading kindness through healthcare). www.hambonepublishing.com.au

Endnotes

1. Henry Mintzberg, Bruce Ahlstrand & Joseph B. Lampel, *Strategy Safari: The complete guide through the wilds of strategic management, (Pearson Education Canada, 2008)*
2. Erica Olsen, *Strategic Planning For Dummies (For Dummies, 2006)*
3. *https://www.iaf-world.org/*
4. A.G. Lafley & Roger L. Martin, *Playing to Win: How Strategy Really Works (Harvard Business Review Press, 2013): 176*
5. Carola Wolf & Steven Floyd, "Strategic Planning Research: Toward a Theory-Driven Agenda," *Journal of Management, 43 (2013): 15, DOI: 10.1177/0149206313478185*
6. John Bryson & Lauren Hamilton Edwards, "Strategic Planning in the Public Sector," *Oxford Research Encyclopedia of Business and Management, May 2017, DOI: 10.1093/acrefore/9780190224851.013.128*
7. Jordan Tama, "How an agency's responsibilities and political context shape government strategic planning: evidence from US Federal agency quadrennial reviews," *Public Management Review, 20:3 (2017): 377-396, DOI: 10.1080/14719037.2017.1285114*
8. Bill Staples, *Transformational Strategy: Facilitation of ToP Participatory Planning, (iUniverse, 2013): 20*
9. John Bryson & Lauren Hamilton Edwards, "Strategic Planning in the Public Sector," *Oxford Research Encyclopedia of Business and Management, May 2017, DOI: 10.1093/acrefore/9780190224851.013.128*
10. Jordan Tama, "How an agency's responsibilities and political context shape government strategic planning: evidence from US Federal agency quadrennial reviews," *Public Management Review, 20:3 (2017): 377-396, DOI: 10.1080/14719037.2017.1285114*
11. Chip Heath & Dan Heath, *Decisive: How to Make Better Choices in Life and Work (Random House Canada, 2013)*
12. Max Mckeown, *The Strategy Book: How to think and act strategically to deliver outstanding results, (FT Press, 2015): 159*
13. Peter Cook, "What if there is no right decision?" May 12, 2020, *https://petercook.com/blog/no-right-decision*
14. John M. Bryson, Lauren Hamilton Edwards & David M. Van Slyke (2018) "Getting strategic about strategic planning research," *Public Management Review, 20:3, 317-339, DOI: 10.1080/14719037.2017.1285111*
15. Jason Fox, *How To Lead A Quest: A Guidebook For Pioneering Leaders (Wiley, 2016)*
16. Hiroyuki Itami, *Mobilizing Invisible Assets, (Harvard University Press, 1987) as quoted in Strategy Safari: The complete guide through the wilds of strategic management, (Pearson Education Canada, 2008), by Mintzeberg et al.*

17. **Max Mckeown,** *The Strategy Book: How to think and act strategically to deliver outstanding results, (FT Press, 2015): 60*

18. **Adam Bryant,** *Quick and Nimble: Lessons from CEOs on How to Create a Culture of Innovation (St. Martin's Griffin, 2014.*

19. **John M. Bryson, Lauren Hamilton Edwards & David M. Van Slyke** *(2018) "Getting strategic about strategic planning research,"* Public Management Review, 20:3, 317-339, DOI: 10.1080/14719037.2017.1285111

20. **Henry Mintzberg,** *The Rise and Fall of Strategic Planning, (Free Press, 1994)*

21. **Max Mckeown,** *The Strategy Book: How to think and act strategically to deliver outstanding results, (FT Press, 2015): 65*

22. **A.G. Lafley & Roger L. Martin,** *Playing to Win: How Strategy Really Works (Harvard Business Review Press, 2013): 3*

23. **J. M. Bryson**, *Strategic Planning for Public and Nonprofit Organizations (Jossey-Bass, 2011): 26*

24. **Carola Wolf & Steven Floyd,** *"Strategic Planning Research: Toward a Theory-Driven Agenda," Journal of Management, 43 (2013): 5, DOI: 10.1177/0149206313478185*

25. **John M. Bryson, Lauren Hamilton Edwards & David M. Van Slyke** *(2018) "Getting strategic about strategic planning research,"* Public Management Review, 20:3, 317-339, DOI: 10.1080/14719037.2017.1285111

26. **John M. Bryson, Lauren Hamilton Edwards & David M. Van Slyke** *(2018) "Getting strategic about strategic planning research,"* Public Management Review, 20:3, 317-339, DOI: 10.1080/14719037.2017.1285111

27. **Max Mckeown**, *The Strategy Book: How to think and act strategically to deliver outstanding results, (FT Press, 2015): 80*

28. **Carola Wolf & Steven Floyd**, *"Strategic Planning Research: Toward a Theory-Driven Agenda," Journal of Management, 43 (2013), DOI: 10.1177/0149206313478185*

29. See for example:
    Eric Weiner, *The Geography Of Genius: A Search For The World's Most Creative Places, From Ancient Athens To Silicone Valley (Simon & Schuster, 2016)*

30. **Peter M. Senge**, *The Fifth Discipline: The Art and Practice of the Learning Organization, (Doubleday/Currency, 1990)*

31. **Peter Economy**, *"This is the Way You Need to Write Down Your Goals for Faster Success," Inc. February 28, 2018,* https://www.inc.com/peter-economy/this-is-way-you-need-to-write-down-your-goals-for-faster-success.html

32. **David Johnston**, *Trust: Twenty Ways to Build a Better Country (Signal, 2018): 167*

33. **Mark Murphy**, *"Neuroscience Explains Why You Need To Write Down Your Goals If You Actually Want To Achieve Them," Forbes, April 2018,* https://www.forbes.com/sites/markmurphy/2018/04/15/neuroscience-explains-why-you-need-to-write-down-your-goals-if-you-actually-want-to-achieve-them/#232921777905

34. **Joel Brockner**, *The Process Matters: Engaging and Equipping People for Success (Princeton University Press, 2017)*

35. **Chip Heath & Dan Heath**, *Decisive: How to Make Better Choices in Life and Work (Random House Canada, 2013)*

36. **Charlotta Siréna & Marko Kohtamäki**, *" Stretching strategic learning to the limit: The interaction between strategic planning and learning," Journal of Business Research, Volume 69, Issue 2 (February 2016): 653-663, https://doi.org/10.1016/j.jbusres.2015.08.035*

37. **Henry Mintzberg, Bruce Ahlstrand & Joseph B. Lampel**, *Strategy Safari: The complete guide through the wilds of strategic management, (Pearson Education Canada, 2008): 229*

38. **Halford Edward Luccock** *(1885—1961)*

39. **Tasha Eurich**, *Insight: Why We're Not as Self-Aware as We Think, and How Seeing Ourselves Clearly Helps Us Succeed at Work and in Life (Sydney: Currency, 2017)*

40. **Jason Fox**, *How To Lead A Quest: A Guidebook For Pioneering Leaders, (Wiley, 2016): 36*

41. **Michael Hyatt**, *Living Forward: A Proven Plan to Stop Drifting and Get the Life You Want, (Baker Books, 2016)*

42. **Tom Wujec**, *"Got a wicked problem? First, tell me how you make toast," filmed June 2013 in Edinburgh, Scotland, TED video, 8:53, https://www.ted.com/talks/tom_wujec_got_a_wicked_problem_first_tell_me_how_you_make_toast*

43. **Greg McKeown**, *Essentialism: The Disciplined Pursuit of Less (Virgin Books, 2014)*

44. **Hilary Hinton "Zig" Ziglar**

45. **David Maister**, *"Strategy Means Saying 'No'," 2006, https://davidmaister.com/articles/strategy-means-saying-no/*

46. **Adam Richardson**, *"Boosting Creativity Through Constraints," Harvard Business Review, June 11, 2013 https://hbr.org/2013/06/boosting-creativity-through-co*

47. **Gary Keller & Jay Papasan**, *The ONE Thing: The Surprisingly Simple Truth Behind Extraordinary Results, (Bard Press, 2013)*

48. **Oliver Wendell Holmes Jr.**

49. **Patrick Lencioni**, *The Five Dysfunctions of a Team: A Leadership Fable (Jossey-Bass, 2002)*

50. **David Lee, Michael McGuire & Jong Ho Kim**, *"Collaboration, strategic plans, and government performance: the case of efforts to reduce homelessness," Public Management Review, 20:3 (2018): 360-376, DOI: 10.1080/14719037.2017.1285113*

51. **Jordan Tama**, *"How an agency's responsibilities and political context shape government strategic planning: evidence from US Federal agency quadrennial reviews," Public Management Review, 20:3 (2017): 377-396, DOI: 10.1080/14719037.2017.1285114*

52. **Åge Johnsen**, *"Impacts of strategic planning and management in municipal government: an analysis of subjective survey and objective production and efficiency measures in Norway," Public Management Review, 20:3, 397-420, DOI: 10.1080/14719037.2017.1285115*

53. Peter Drucker
54. **Tom Peters**, *"When you're looking for a way, any map will do,"* Chicago Tribune (February 13, 1995), *https://www.chicagotribune.com/news/ct-xpm-1995-02-13-9502130021-story.html*
55. **A.G. Lafley & Roger L. Martin**, *Playing to Win: How Strategy Really Works (Harvard Business Review Press, 2013): 4*
56. **Richard Rumelt**, *Good Strategy/Bad Strategy: The Difference and Why It Matters (Profile Books Ltd, 2017)*
57. **D. Levy**, *"Chaos Theory and Strategy: Theory, Application, and Managerial Implications."* Strategic Management Journal (15, 1994: 167-178) *as quoted by Henry Mintzberg, Bruce Ahlstrand & Joseph B. Lampel, Strategy Safari: The complete guide through the wilds of strategic management, (Pearson Education Canada, 2008)*
58. **Roger L. Martin**, *"The Big Lie of Strategic Planning,"* Harvard Business Review (January-February 2014) *https://hbr.org/2014/01/the-big-lie-of-strategic-planning*
59. **Max Mckeown**, *The Strategy Book: How to think and act strategically to deliver outstanding results, (FT Press, 2015): 36*
60. **Jason Fox**, *How To Lead A Quest: A Guidebook For Pioneering Leaders (Wiley, 2016)*
61. **Henri Lipmanowicz & Keith McCandless**, *The Surprising Power of Liberating Structures: Simple Rules to Unleash A Culture of Innovation (Liberating Structures Press, 2014)*
62. **Michael Cowley & Ellen Domb**, *Beyond Strategic Vision: Effective Corporate Action with Hoshin Planning, (Butterworth-Heinemann, 1997): 3*
63. **Bert George, Sebastian Desmidt, Eva Cools & Anita Prinzie**, *"Cognitive styles, user acceptance and commitment to strategic plans in public organizations: an empirical analysis,"* Public Management Review, 20:3, (2018): 340-359
64. **Max Mckeown**, *The Strategy Book: How to think and act strategically to deliver outstanding results, (FT Press, 2015): 144*
65. **Carola Wolf & Steven Floyd**, *"Strategic Planning Research: Toward a Theory-Driven Agenda,"* Journal of Management, 43 (2013): 19, DOI: 10.1177/0149206313478185
66. **Bill Staples**, *Transformational Strategy: Facilitation of ToP Participatory Planning, (iUniverse, 2013)*
67. **Michael Wilkinson**, *The Executive Guide to Facilitating Strategy (Leadership Strategies Publishing, 2011)*
68. **John M. Bryson, Lauren Hamilton Edwards & David M. Van Slyke** (2018) *"Getting strategic about strategic planning research,"* Public Management Review, 20:3, 317-339, DOI: 10.1080/14719037.2017.1285111
69. **Hal B. Gregerson**, *Questions Are The Answers: A Breakthrough Approach to Your Most Vexing Problems at Work and in Life, (Harper Business, 2018)*
70. **Nilofer Merchant**, *The Power of Onlyness: Make Your Wild Ideas Mighty Enough to Dent the World, (Viking, 2017): 129*

71. **Chip Conley**, *Wisdom at Work: The Making of a Modern Elder, (Currency, 2018): 90*

72. **Warren Berger**, *A More Beautiful Question: The Power of Inquiry to Spark Breakthrough Ideas, Bloombury USA, 2014): 5*

73. **Amanda Lang**, *The Power of Why, (Collins, 2014)*

74. **Tim Ferriss**, *Tool of Titans: The Tactics, Routines, and Habits of Billionaires, Icons, and World-Class Performers, (Houghton Mifflin Harcourt, 2016)*
    Tim Ferriss. *(January 29, 2017) Asking Dumb Questions Is a Smart Move. Retrieved from https://www.youtube.com/watch?v=iE4jASYcopo*

75. **Edgar H. Schein**, *Humble Consulting: How to Provide Real Help Faster (Berrett-Koehler Publishers, 2016): 40*

76. **Hal B. Gregerson**, *Questions Are The Answers: A Breakthrough Approach to Your Most Vexing Problems at Work and in Life, (Harper Business, 2018)*

77. **Edgar H. Schein**, *Humble Inquiry: The Gentle Art of Asking and Telling (Berrett-Koehler Publishers, 2013): 44*

78. **Richard Rumelt**, *Good Strategy/Bad Strategy: The Difference and Why It Matters (Profile Books Ltd, 2017)*

79. **Stephen R. Covey**. *The 7 Habits of Highly Effective People: Powerful Lessons in Personal Change (Simon & Schuster, 2013)*

80. *See for example:*
    Resources from the International Association for Public Participation, https://www.iap2.org; Bang the Table, https://www.bangthetable.com; and https://rebeccasutherns.com/stakeholder-engagement/

81. *A similar tool is used to plan broader public participation ot identify those impacted by a decision and those with the power to make it happen.*

82. *For more details, refer to the "IAP2 Spectrum of Public Participation," https://www.iap2.org/page/pillars*

83. **Steve Jobs**. *"The Next Insanely Great Thing." Interview by Gary Wolf. Wired, February 1996, https://www.wired.com/1996/02/jobs-2/*

84. *Some examples:*
    Yuval Noah Harari, *21 Lessons for the 21st Century, (Signal, 2018)*
    Matt Church, *Next: Thoughts about tomorrow you can talk about today, (Thought Leaders Publishing, 2018)*
    Authors such as Douglas Coupland and Faith Popcorn, highlighting the era-specific nature of this work.

85. **Benjamin Franklin**, *The Autobiography of Benjamin Franklin, (J. Parson's, 1793): 48*

86. **Kieran Flanagan & Dan Gregory**, *Forever Skills: The 12 Skills to Futureproof Yourself, Your Team and Your Kids, (Wiley, 2019): 149*

87. *SOAR, http://soar-strategy.com/*

88. **James Clear**, *https://jamesclear.com/*

89. *TOC Origins, Centre for Theory of Change, https://www.theoryofchange.org/what-is-theory-of-change/toc-background/toc-origins/*

90. *For example: Centre for Theory of Change, https://www.theoryof-change.org/; tools4dev, http://www.tools4dev.org/resources/theory-of-change-vs-logical-framework-whats-the-difference-in-practice/*

91. **Bill Staples**, *Transformational Strategy: Facilitation of ToP Participatory Planning, (iUniverse, 2013): 135*

92. **Bill Staples**, *Transformational Strategy: Facilitation of ToP Participatory Planning, (iUniverse, 2013)*

93. **Sam Kaner**, *Facilitator's Guide to Participatory Decision-Making (Jossey-Bass, 2014)*

94. *See for example: Centre for Theory of Change, Theory of Change Online (TOCO) https://www.theoryofchange.org/toco-software/*

95. **John Izzo & Jeff VanderWeilen**, *The Purpose Revolution: How Leaders Create Engagement and Competitive Advantage in an Age of Social Good (Berrett-Koehler Publishers, 2018)*

96. *With thanks to Michael Wilkinson whose work on positioning in The Executive Guide to Facilitating Strategy (Leadership Strategies Publishing, 2011) has influenced mine. https://michaelthefacilitator.com/*

97. **Edwin A. Locke & Gary P. Latham**, *A Theory of Goal Setting & Task Performance, (Pearson College Div., 1990)*

98. **Lisa D. Ordóñez, Maurice E. Schweitzer, Adam D. Galinsky, and Max H. Bazerman.** *"Goals Gone Wild: The Systematic Side Effects of Over-Prescribing Goal Setting." Harvard Business School Working Paper, No. 09-083 (January 2009)*

99. **Oliver Burkeman**, *The Antidote: Happiness for People Who Can't Stand Positive Thinking (Faber & Faber, 2013)*

100. **D. Christopher Kayes**, *Destructive Goal Pursuit: The Mt. Everest Disaster, (Palgrave Macmillan, 2006)*

101. **Stephen M. Shapiro**, *Goal-Free Living: How to Have the Life You Want NOW!, (Wiley, 2006)*

102. **Brian Tracy**, *Goals!: How to Get Everything You Want -- Faster Than You Ever Thought Possible, (Berrett-Koehler Publishers, 2010)*

103. **A.G. Lafley & Roger L. Martin**, *Playing to Win: How Strategy Really Works (Harvard Business Review Press, 2013)*

104. **Richard Rumelt**, *Good Strategy/Bad Strategy: The Difference and Why It Matters (Profile Books Ltd, 2017): 12*

105. **Tasha Eurich**, *Insight: Why We're Not as Self-Aware as We Think, and How Seeing Ourselves Clearly Helps Us Succeed at Work and in Life (Currency, 2017)*

106. **Chip Heath & Dan Heath**, *Decisive: How to Make Better Choices at Life and Work (Random House Canada, 2013): 3*

107. **Henry Mintzberg**, *The Rise and Fall of Strategic Planning, (Free Press, 1994): 300*

108. **A.G. Lafley & Roger L. Martin**, *Playing to Win: How Strategy Really Works (Harvard Business Review Press, 2013)*

109. **A.G. Lafley & Roger L. Martin**, *Playing to Win: How Strategy Really Works (Harvard Business Review Press, 2013)*

110. **James Clear**, *The Goal is Not the Point. https://jamesclear.com/treasure-hunt*

111. **Michael Wilkinson**, *2011. The Executive Guide to Facilitating Strategy. Leadership Strategies Publishing.*

112. **Covey Stephen, R, A. Roger, Merrill and Rebecca R. Merrill**, *1995. First Things First: To Live, to Love, to Learn, to Leave a Legacy. (Simon & Schuster 1995)*

113. **Bill Staples**, *Transformational Strategy: Facilitation of ToP Participatory Planning, (iUniverse, 2013)*

114. **Tom Kelley & David Kelley**, *Creative Confidence: Unleashing the Creative Potential Within Us All, (Currency, 2013)*
Ed Catmull, *Creativity, Inc.: Overcoming the Unseen Forces That Stand in the Way of True Inspiration, (Random House Canada, 2014)*
David Usher, *Let the Elephants Run, Unlock Your Creativity and Change Everything, (House of Anansi Press, 2015)*
Elizabeth Gilbert, *Big Magic: Creative Living Beyond Fear, (Riverhead Books, 2015)*
Tom Kelley & Jonathan Littman, *The Ten Faces of Innovation: IDEO's Strategies for Beating the Devil's Advocate and Driving Creativity Throughout Your Organization, (Currency, 2015)*
Tina Seelig, *Ingenius: A Crash Course on Creativity, (HarperOne, 2012)*
Eric Weiner, *The Geography of Genius: A Search for the World's Most Creative Places from Ancient Athens to Silicon Valley, (Simon & Schuster, 2016)*
Scott Barry Kaufman & Carolyn Gregoire, *Wired to Create: Unraveling the Mysteries of the Creative Mind, (Random House Canada, 2015)*
Jeff Dyer, Hal Gregersen, Clayton M. Christensen, *The Innovator's DNA: Mastering the Five Skills of Disruptive Innovators, (Harvard Business Review Press, 2011)*
Linda Hill, Greg Bandeau, Emily Truelove & Kent Lineback, *Collective Genius: The Art and Practice of Leading Innovation, (Harvard Business Review Press, 2014)*

115. **Cal Newport**, *Deep Work: Rules for Focused Success in a Distracted World, (Grand Central Publishing, 2016)*

116. **Alex Soojung-Kim Pang**, *Rest: Why You Get More Done When You Work Less, (Basic Books, 2016)*

117. **Chip Heath & Dan Heath**, *Decisive: How to Make Better Choices in Life and Work (Random House Canada, 2013)*

118. **Michael Cowley & Ellen Domb**, *Beyond Strategic Vision: Effective Corporate Action with Hoshin Planning, (Butterworth-Heinemann, 1997)*

119. **Chris McChesney & Sean Covey**, *The 4 Disciplines of Execution (Simon & Schuster Ltd, 2015)*

120. **A.G. Lafley & Roger L. Martin**, *Playing to Win: How Strategy Really Works (Harvard Business Review Press, 2013)*
A.G. Lafley & Roger L. Martin, *Playing to Win: How Strategy Really Works (Harvard Business Review Press, 2013): 36*

121. *We see the same thing with telecommunications companies and many other subscription services where they make cancelling your commitment a headache for customers, on purpose.*

122. **Michael Cowley & Ellen Domb**, *Beyond Strategic Vision: Effective Corporate Action with Hoshin Planning, (Butterworth-Heinemann, 1997)*

123. *You could dig deeper here into what the group is looking for in a good idea. High leverage ideas that accomplish multiple objectives at once are the favourite.*

124. *Some facilitators use an equation for calculating the appropriate number of dots to distribute per person: the number of total ideas divided by three, plus one. Do with it what you will.*

125. **Jason Fox**, *How To Lead A Quest: A Guidebook For Pioneering Leaders (Wiley, 2016)*

126. **Henry Mintzberg**, *The Rise and Fall of Strategic Planning, (Free Press, 1994)*

127. **Henry Mintzberg**, *The Rise and Fall of Strategic Planning, (Free Press, 1994): 256*

128. **David Johnston**, *Trust: Twenty Ways to Build a Better Country (Signal, 2018)*

129. **Henry Mintzberg, Bruce Ahlstrand & Joseph B. Lampel**, *Strategy Safari: The complete guide through the wilds of strategic management, (Pearson Education Canada, 2008)*

130. **A.G. Lafley & Roger L. Martin**, *Playing to Win: How Strategy Really Works (Harvard Business Review Press, 2013): 215*

131. **Alicia McKay**, *From Strategy to Action: A Guide to Getting Shit Done In The Public Sector, (2019), https://www.aliciamckay.co.nz/*

132. **Max Mckeown**, *The Strategy Book: How to think and act strategically to deliver outstanding results, (FT Press, 2015): 161*

133. **Joel Brockner**, *The Process Matters: Engaging and Equipping People for Success (Princeton University Press, 2017)*

134. **Chris McChesney & Sean Covey**, *The 4 Disciplines of Execution (Simon & Schuster Ltd, 2015): 22*

135. **Edgar H. Schein**, *Humble Consulting: How to Provide Real Help Faster (Berrett-Koehler Publishers, 2016)*

136. **Jason Fox**, *How To Lead A Quest: A Guidebook For Pioneering Leaders (Wiley, 2016)*

137. **Robert Bly, Iron John**: *A Book About Men (Da Capo Press, 2015): 8*

138. **Chris McChesney & Sean Covey**, *The 4 Disciplines of Execution (Simon & Schuster Ltd, 2015)*

139. **Michael Cowley & Ellen Domb**, *Beyond Strategic Vision: Effective Corporate Action with Hoshin Planning, (Butterworth-Heinemann, 1997): 9*

140. **James Clear**, *The Magic of Committing to a Specific Goal. https://jamesclear.com/magic-of-committing*

141. **James Clear**, *Atomic Habits: An Easy & Proven Way to Build Good Habits & Break Bad Ones (Avery, 2018)*

142. **Max Mckeown**, *The Strategy Book: How to think and act strategically to deliver outstanding results, (FT Press, 2015): 157*

143. **James Clear**, *Atomic Habits: An Easy & Proven Way to Build Good Habits & Break Bad Ones (Avery, 2018): Chapter 1. Also at https://jamesclear.com/goals-systems.*

144. **Bill Staples**, *Transformational Strategy: Facilitation of ToP Participatory Planning, (iUniverse, 2013): 187*

145. **Edgar H. Schein**, *Humble Consulting: How to Provide Real Help Faster (Berrett-Koehler Publishers, 2016): 64*

146. **Gary Keller & Jay Papasan**, *The ONE Thing: The Surprisingly Simple Truth Behind Extraordinary Results, (Bard Press, 2013)*

147. **Chris McChesney & Sean Covey**, *The 4 Disciplines of Execution (Simon & Schuster Ltd, 2015)*

148. **Gary Keller & Jay Papasan**, *The ONE Thing: The Surprisingly Simple Truth Behind Extraordinary Results, (Bard Press, 2013)*

149. **Henry Mintzberg, Bruce Ahlstrand & Joseph B. Lampel**, *Strategy Safari: The complete guide through the wilds of strategic management, (Pearson Education Canada, 2008)*

150. **Henry Mintzberg**, *The Rise and Fall of Strategic Planning, (Free Press, 1994): 226*

151. **Max Mckeown**, *The Strategy Book: How to think and act strategically to deliver outstanding results, (FT Press, 2015): 165*

152. **James Clear**, *Atomic Habits: An Easy & Proven Way to Build Good Habits & Break Bad Ones, (Avery, 2018)*
    Charles Duhigg, *The Power of Habit: Why We Do What We Do in Life and Business, (Anchor Canada, 2014)*
    BJ Fogg, *Tiny Habits: The Small Changes That Change Everything, (Houghton Mifflin Harcourt, 2019)*

153. **Chris McChesney & Sean Covey**, *The 4 Disciplines of Execution (Simon & Schuster Ltd, 2015)*

154. **Michael Cowley & Ellen Domb**, *Beyond Strategic Vision: Effective Corporate Action with Hoshin Planning, (Butterworth-Heinemann, 1997)*